THE REDEMPTION
OF ALL THINGS

BETH MARIE EVANS

To
LeAnn,
May your walk with
God be ordered as you
read,
Beth Marie Evans
3/30/19

In Memory of J. T. Pugh

Who Resisted Unto Blood

Cover design by Utopia Upshire

All scriptures cited in the text, unless otherwise noted, are taken from the King James Version of the Bible. All Hebrew and Greek translations of word in scripture, unless otherwise noted, are taken from Strong's Exhaustive Concordance.

Fifty percent of all proceeds earned from sales of this book, excluding cost of printing, will be given to Foreign Missions towards the global vision of the UPCI to take the whole Gospel of Jesus Christ to the whole world.

Copyright © 2018 by Beth Marie Evans

Library of Congress Control Number: 2018907578

ISBN: 978-0-9771212-1-2

Published in the United States by
Triumphant Through Truth Publications

Printed in the United States
by Pentecostal Publishing House
8855 Dunn Rd
Hazelwood MO 63042
(636) 229-7900

Acknowledgments

There are many who will play a part in fulfilling the purpose of this book, including those who are reading the following. Fifty percent of all proceeds, excluding printing cost, from sales of this book will go to missions. I would also like to give credit where credit is due to:

Noel Cornejo, for his initial and excellent work on the book cover, locating photos, and his photo of myself on the back cover.

Kathie Wellman, for her excellence in editing, taking the time to endorse this work, and for introducing me to Utopia Upshire.

Utopia Upshire, of Upshire Enterprises, for her excellence in vision, which enabled me to connect title, cover, and manuscript. And for the finalization of a beautiful cover design.

Denise Horn, who provided valuable information about the Answers in Genesis website, which saved me hours of research.

Dedication

This book is dedicated to our Lord and Savior, Jesus Christ. My first book, *Gaining Control of Your Mind Through the Mind of Christ*, was written as a result of the deliverance I received by entering into covenant with Him. This second book has been written as a result of revelation received that has enabled me to keep that blood covenant.

I cannot fail to mention my love and thankfulness for my home Church, International Christian Fellowship, Bishop, and First Lady Vicki Gonzalez, Pastors Rick, and Angela Gonzalez. I also want to express gratitude for the privilege of attending the Passing the Mantle Conference. I honor the memory of Jack Yontz. I also, acknowledge Pastor Robert Boettcher, and the Bartlett Pentecostal Church. It was at the Passing the Mantle Conference, while listening to a message preached by Rev. J. T. Pugh, that I was inspired to write this book. Of course, I cannot fail to mention my husband, Danny Evans, who has brought such positive change into my life. Along with my children, Terry Lopez, Scott Rexford, and my grandchildren; all give me purpose, and the incentive to pursue a rich heritage for the next generation.

Table of Contents

Foreword

s an honor to once again present the reader with a literary work by
th Evans, formerly, Beth Rexford. In her first treatise, Beth takes us
a journey of self discovery as she challenged us to embrace the
actical, yet life changing principles, that make the Christian life a
werful testimony of living with the "mind of Christ".

this book, not only does Beth call out the "The Many Faces of Fear",
t she also presents the reader with a well researched Biblical
ronology of the work of fear in the human heart.

ue to her style, and personal journey; she not just informs, but also
ovides real answers to the dilemma of fear. She does this by reminding
that a life in Christ is a covenant with powerful implications that
ust be undergirded in the fear that we must all wholeheartedly
ibrace and let grow in our lives; the fear of the Lord.

great read, full of wisdom!!!

c S. Gonzalez
shop, and Founder of International Christian Fellowship
iicago Metro

Intent

The intent of this book is to transmit revelatory understanding of how the spirit of fear is strategically used by the enemy to steal our faith by subtly working against our carnal mind, which is inherent in our fallen nature. Should we allow ourselves to be robbed of our faith; we will be unable to keep our covenant with God, who is a maker and keeper of Covenants. The serpent was successful in using doubt to cause Adam and Eve to fall. My hope and prayer is that he will be unsuccessful with the saints of the living God.

After I was inspired to write this book, I went through a traumatic situation that was totally out of my control. It was brought about as a result of choices made by others, which negatively affected people I hold near and dear to me. And was the worst thing I had experienced since entering into a covenant with God through baptism in His name, and receiving the Holy Ghost. This situation compelled me to begin a 40 day fast, which was difficult, and took a toll on my physical health, but was beneficial to my spiritual well-being. On the 39th day of the fast, God spoke to me regarding this book, which I had already been inspired to write. God spoke to me, and I quote, "I want you to tell my people how their fear is causing them to break their covenant with Me". It was interesting to me that ownership was given to fear. Scripture teaches us that fear is a spirit. I have since come to the understanding that we can embrace, and be led by the spirit of fear; instead of embracing, and being led by the Holy Ghost. The spirit of fear is in direct opposition to the Spirit of Truth, and can be described as faith in something that is not real. Scripture tells us of those who were in great fear where no fear was. In reality, God had already scattered the bones of their enemies. With faith, we can have victory over fear.

3

Faith can be summed up as this: the belief that no matter what situation we find ourselves in, God will always do right by us. We must not allow ourselves to become offended at God when things don't go our way or we suffer loss. Fear can be overcome with truth, faith, and love. Not the world's love, but God's perfect love. We should continually ask God to impart wisdom to us, which will enable us to discern between what is true and what is false. Listening to fear will cause us to doubt God's Word. It is my intention to shed light on the spirit of fear with the Word of God. When a light is turned on in a dark room, it exposes what is in that room. God, who is light, will expose fear for what it is, and help us overcome our fallen nature.

He Thought of You

As He set His face towards Gethsemane that day,
He thought of you every step of the way.
As He healed, delivered, and set captives free,
With everlasting love, He thought of you and me.

As He became the perfect sacrifice,
As He paid the ultimate price,
As He made His way to Calvary,
He became sin for you and me.

He wore a crown of thorns to purify our minds.
Through His power alone, healing we will find.
Through His sacrifice made at Calvary,
Came healing of the soul for all humanity.

Beth Marie Evans

Chapter One
Fear Enters Paradise

To overcome fear, we must diligently seek God in good times and in bad. We cannot allow the enemy to capitalize on anything in our lives or be influenced into believing things about God that aren't true. If we are led by the Spirit of Truth, He will lead us into all Truth. Wisdom from God will enable us to discern between what is true, and what is false. We need wisdom from God, not earthly, worldly wisdom. Only wisdom from above can help us to negotiate our way through deception, and the snares of the enemy. God will impart His wisdom to those who ask Him (see James 1:5). Wisdom and understanding will enable us to conquer fear and its negative effects on our lives. Fear and unbelief lead to sin because if we don't believe in the principles of God's Word, we will not obey them. When we allow fear to control our emotions, it can result in a negative reaction, and actions that go against God's Word.

In times of doubt, we must call upon God. We need faith in God's Word as our foundation for life. Doubt, which opens the door for fear, will negatively affect how we react to situations. Consider the following illustration: I live in an old farmhouse in the Midwest. During the summer of 2005, I was having a problem with bats getting into the house. I am generally not afraid of these animals. Over the years, I have grown accustomed to seeing these small brown bats from time to time. They are typically docile creatures. One night, a bat flew into the room acting differently than any I had seen before. It did not seem to be affected by the light in the room. It kept circling the room and came a little too close for comfort. I reacted by hitting him with the chair I was sitting on and killing him. Again, I

usually don't mind these little creatures. In reality, they are harmless and beneficial; having the ability to eat their weight in insects in one night. When this one acted differently than the others I had seen the past, I was afraid. Fear of anything or anyone that is different from us can have the same effect on us spiritually. Fear is the underlying cause of racism, which is a great evil in the eyes of God. Fear can keep us from venturing out into the unknown, and keep us from fulfilling the Great Commission. It can play on our human emotions, using negative past experiences to separate us from others and God. We cannot do the will of God if we are bound by fear.

In short, if given dominion, fear will keep us from keeping our covenant with our covenant making and keeping God. Our relationship with God calls us to walk in newness of life. This, in addition to the Great Commission, is the will of God for us. However, all too often the memories of our sinful past prevent us from enjoying our blessed future, and the abundant life God purchased for us at Calvary. We must choose to believe in the power of the cross, and believe what the Word of God tells us.

When we think and act according to our human emotions and reasoning, it is not likely that we will venture out of our comfort zone. Fear will cause us to rationalize situations according to worldly wisdom, and by what has happened to us in the past, which is the motivating factor in humanism. Humanism is a mindset that puts faith in man, and one's own abilities, not in God, or His ability to do the impossible.

Trusting God means that we believe He will always do right by us, even when we don't like or understand our situation. No matter what new situation comes our way, we must choose to believe in God, and pray for understanding. We will not always get an answer, but God will give us peace when we are living in accordance with His Word. The peace of God is better than an answer. When doubt is allowed to enter in by our human reasoning, our peace is taken, and our strength is gone. When we don't have the strength to fight, it is easy to fall into sin.

In fact, a vicious cycle is created by doubting God's Word, then falling into sin, which usually causes something bad to happen. When we are faced with the result of our bad choices, shame sets in to keep us from the source of our strength, which is God. We must break out of this cycle (should we find ourselves there) by having a Holy Ghost break down. In other words, find an altar of repentance from the things that dragged us down, and keep the fire of Holy Ghost burning through fervent prayer. We must continually walk in the Spirit. Those who won't be led by the Spirit will easily be led astray by their own lust into unbelief. If we put faith in the past, shame (a human emotion), along with fear (a spirit), will separate us from God.

If we allow doubt to enter our minds as a result of hurt and discouragement, not turning towards God during the storms of our lives, the next thing we know...we end up unprotected in enemy territory. Also, we must have compassion on those who have been beaten down by the storms of life, and help those who have fallen, and are suffering the harmful effects of shame and fear. If we fail to have compassion for the fallen, we are in opposition to God's commandment to restore. Our enemy does not want restoration. He will use whatever means possible to prevent it. We cannot let fear prevent our love for others, no matter who they are. Individually we are not called to reach out to everyone, but when an opportunity presents itself, we must wisely and boldly speak the Word of God.

Fear Enters Paradise

We do not need to fear our enemy. He can't do anything but intimidate and deceive. We must remember that we have been given all power to tread upon serpents and scorpions. We have been given ALL power over the enemy, and nothing shall harm us. The enemy will attempt to get us into a position where we doubt God and His power. Should we happen to fall into sin, or should there be some shortcoming, we may also begin to doubt God's love for us. The enemy wants us to question God. Once we start to doubt God, we will try to take control of situations, and not depend on God. This is how humanism evolved. Humanism and its mindset will separate us from God. While sin results in a breach of a covenant with God, fear will attempt to prevent the repairing of that breach that God desires us to have. When we choose not to believe that God wants to forgive us, we are standing against everything He did at Calvary.

Humanism originated in the Garden of Eden. Humanism is a way of thinking that is in opposition towards God. It is a way of thinking that leaves God out, and lets satan in. It should be noted that scripture defines fear as a spirit. However, unbelief is the result of making a willful choice to listen to the voice of the enemy, rather than the Word of God. Fear is a device the enemy can use to get us to break our covenant relationship with God. The plan of satan is to get us to embrace his way of thinking, when enticed by him, instead of being led by, and living according to God's Word.

His most significant advantage over us is our own thinking and our failures. The reason why our failures have such power over us is shame and pride. However, we want to look at it, shame and pride work against us in the same way because they both come from a mindset or stronghold that is a result of mentally giving self (one's actions) or a situation more power

9

than God's Word. God has made His Word more powerful than His name. In the beginning was the Word...David wrote in Psalm 138 that God has magnified His Word above His name. His Word says there is forgiveness of sins for those who genuinely repent. We must choose to believe in the Spirit of Truth, and reject the spirit of fear.

The Holy Ghost has power over anything the enemy can bring our way. He literally is the presence of our departed Savior. The Spirit of God is love, joy, peace, long-suffering, gentleness, goodness, faith, meekness, and temperance (see Galatians 5:22-23). The enemy has none of these attributes; he is hatred, negativity, confusion, contention, destruction, wickedness, fear, hopelessness, and ignorance.

When our minds are open to his influence, we will be subject to these elements of darkness. The devil knows that he has no hope for reprieve, and is destined for the lake of fire. He desires to destroy God's most treasured creation, mankind. In this hour he is attempting to destroy His bride, the Church. The devil hopes to accomplish this with fear, hoping we will allow our faith to waver. Our enemy's strategy is to get us to break our covenant with God through unbelief and disobedience. Working through tragedies, past experiences, and things that others have done, the enemy has had some temporary success. We must be vigilant because he knows our weaknesses. We must exercise our faith, and be obedient to God. Faith and obedience will be required, if we are to stand in the evil days to come.

If we don't believe God will fulfill His promises to us; it is not likely that we will stay faithful to Him when the going gets rough. When things get rough, we need to turn to God. We need to pray. We need to make thankfulness a daily practice. We want to make our covenant with God a sure covenant. II Peter 1:10

assures us that if we will be diligent in our faith, practicing brotherly love, kindness, godliness, self-control, patience, and learning, we will never fail. We need the wisdom, knowledge, and understanding that come from the Spirit of God to help us fulfill His covenant. When tragedy strikes, we should not turn to other things or people. We need to pray through, and wait on God. If we fail to trust God, trying to take control of situations, things usually get worse. The farther we get from God, the deeper into deception we go. The spirit of fear has free reign in deception. And this is where the enemy wants us to be.

It has been the goal of the devil, since the day God created man, to prevent mankind from keeping his covenant with God. The enemy spoke confusion regarding God's Word to Eve to get her to eat the forbidden fruit. According to what is written, Eve was deceived, and Adam chose to rebel against God's Word. These actions caused God's first covenant with man to be broken. They allowed doubt to cause them to disobey God's Word, which led to the fall of man. Likewise, a lack of faith will cause us to doubt God. The end result will be unfaithfulness.

A covenant relationship begins when we are baptized in His name. This is when we put on Christ. Then we are instructed to allow His Spirit to counsel, teach, remold, and form us into His image. This cannot happen without prayer and consecration. If we do not pray and learn His Word, we cannot know Him. This is usually where the problem starts. We need godly attributes. If we are to have these, we need the mind of Christ; without His Spirit, Name, and Word, we cannot put on Christ.

If the enemy can get us to doubt the Word of God, we will lose the battle for our souls. It is possible for this to happen when we choose to believe things that are not in accordance with God's Word, or sound good to us, and when we willfully choose to go our own way. However, in the absence of presumptuous sin, satan is often successful in using tragedy, loss, and personal failures, to draw people away from God. It is most unfortunate when this happens to those who have heard His Word, bear His name, and are in covenant relationship with Him. In the midst of a crisis, we should seek God for help instead of taking matters into our own hands. Our lack of faith in God leaves us open to the enemies' influence. We need the influence of the Holy Ghost when we are hurt, disappointed or angry. If we are not walking in the Spirit, we leave ourselves open to the stumbling blocks the enemy will attempt to put in our path. A few of these are rebellion, bitterness, and shame. These enemies to our soul gain momentum and do the most damage when we are not diligent in seeking God during times of tribulation. They will always cause us to make destructive and sometimes life-changing decisions.

Rebellion, bitterness, and shame were evident at the fall of man, and are a result of being fear motivated instead of Spirit motivated. When God asked Adam if he had eaten from the tree that he had been forbidden to eat from, Adam's reply was, *"The woman whom thou gavest to be with me, she gave me of the tree, and I did eat" (Genesis 3:12)*. In this statement, Adam blamed God, and Eve, hence bitterness and rebellion. It is safe to concur that Adam did so because he was ashamed. Shame is a stumbling block, which prevents many from taking responsibility for their own actions. It is a human emotion that fosters self-hatred and leads to more destructive and sinful behavior. Eve blamed the devil, giving him power in her life, and not taking responsibility for her actions. We are told in James 1:14, that we are tempted, drawn away by our own lust, and then enticed. The only way out of this mental trap is to repent, turning away from sin, continually turning towards God, and

12

His ways. He has the power to set us free, but we must be determined to forgive. The same applies to all three aspects of an unforgiving heart: bitterness (a grudge against others), rebellion (a grudge against God), and shame (a grudge against self). Shame is a result of not believing in God's power to forgive. Shame is another aspect of pride that hinders repentance.

Things went downhill for mankind for quite some time until the birth, ministry, and crucifixion of Jesus. Although many had faith that was accounted to them for righteousness (a great cloud of witnesses), there was no Savior. They had to rest on the promises of God. The children of Israel wavered in their faith, and never saw the Promised Land. We may think of the Promised Land as being heaven. And while heaven is our desired destination, Paul said, *"There remaineth therefore a rest to the people of God"* (Hebrews 4:9). The children of Israel did not have rest from their past in Egypt, but feared, and did not put faith in the Word of God. It would seem they never overcame their slave mentality. They saw God as a cruel taskmaster. Their knowledge of God never went beyond religion.

They never were able to embrace the abundant life God wanted to give them. Their unbelief kept them from entering in, and many walked in the wilderness until those who doubted God had died off. If we are to fear anything, it should be to suffer their fate. They could not withstand the testing of God, in spite of His goodness and miracles. God wants us to have abundant life here on earth. We must learn to rest on His promises so He can do the miraculous through us.

It can be difficult to wait on God during a trial, but we must continue to believe, choosing not to be overcome by doubt and fear. Even in the lives of those who are living for God, we sometimes see tragedy. We cannot live for God believing that we will never suffer the effects of living in a fallen world, basing our desire to do what is right on the hope that nothing bad will ever happen to us. God will undoubtedly deliver, and give peace in the middle of any storm, but we will have tribulation. Jesus let us know this, but He also promised never to leave or forsake us. We have to learn to lean on God when we feel our strength is gone. If we learn to lean on God, we will have the strength to stand. When we are at our weakest point, leaning on God will enable us to stand through any storm life brings our way.

Like the majestic eagle, we will be able to fly in the face of the storms of life. Fear must be put under our feet if we are to overcome. It may be that we have not counted the cost. Therefore, we are afraid to stay in the battle. Instead of drawing closer to God, believing He will deliver us, we seek our own way out. It is a fact that in any war there are casualties, but we will be victorious if we stay in the battle. We are promised victory, and we can be sure that we will gain more than we will ever lose.

The life of Jesus is our prime example. He overcame the world, winning the victory over death, hell, and the grave. He stood against every trial that came His way. Even though His mortal body was killed, not a bone in it was broken. His Spirit never died, and He retained a heavenly body with an eternal Kingdom. We are promised the same, and less is required of us. We are not required to pay for our repented sin. Through God's covenant, His blood has washed it away. He became sin for us so that we can live.

He did nothing wrong, and was mistreated by the very ones He came to save. If we are to be like Him, we must expect to carry a cross before we receive a crown. The Bible says, *"Yea, and all that will live godly in Christ Jesus shall suffer persecution"* (2 Tim 3:12-13). If we live righteously, we will suffer some kind of persecution. However, in our fallen world, trouble will also come to those who don't live for God.

Peter told the Church that we shouldn't be surprised when trials come. In fact, he said that we should expect to suffer for doing what is right at times. Trials are a part of life. In this life, we can expect tribulation, with or without a relationship with God. According to the Word of God, it is better to suffer for doing what is right than it is to suffer for doing what is wrong, but this perspective doesn't make sense to the carnal mind. It will cause the carnal man to doubt God, and this it the beginning of rebellion. Many blame God for everything. They never stop to consider that mankind has been driven from God's presence because of wicked acts that God cannot tolerate. Much of the evil in the world is due to mankind's greed and hatred towards his fellow man, and it is wrong to blame God for not micromanaging the wicked deeds of men who rebel against His Word, but we can be sure that God will judge every act, be it good or bad.

God's Word plainly states that if we do what is right, we will be accepted. And if not, sin lies at the door. This is played out many times throughout scripture in the lives of men, beginning with Cain and Abel. We have the Spirit of God available to us in a way they did not. The Spirit-filled man should realize that trouble comes with the territory. I Peter 2:20-21 says *"For what glory is it, if, when ye be buffeted for your faults, ye shall take it patiently? but if, when ye do well, and suffer for it, ye take it patiently, this is acceptable with God. For even hereunto were ye called: because Christ also suffered for us, leaving us an example, that ye should follow his steps"*. We must believe that God knows the outcome of every situation. We will not benefit from leaning on our own understanding. Therefore, even when we don't understand the things we are going through, we must believe He has a deeper plan at work. If we are in covenant with Him, His plan is to prosper us. He has chosen us. It is up to us to be led by His Spirit.

His Word says that His thoughts are above our thoughts, and His ways are above our ways. We will go through trials in this life, with or without God. Jesus has given us His reassurance that He has already overcome the things of this world for us. He has made it possible for us to overcome this world when we utilize the power He has made available to us. When we choose to believe that God can and will deliver us, our faith will be increased.

I Peter 4:12-16 says, *"Beloved, think it not strange concerning the fiery trial which is to try you, as though some strange thing happened unto you: But rejoice, inasmuch as ye are partakers of Christ's sufferings; that, when his glory shall be revealed, ye may be glad also with exceeding joy. If ye be reproached for the name of Christ, happy are ye; for the spirit of glory and of God resteth upon you: on their part he is evil spoken of, but on your part he is glorified. But let none of you suffer as a murderer, or as a thief, or as an evildoer, or as a busybody in other men's matters. Yet if any man suffer as a Christian, let him not be ashamed; but let him glorify God on this behalf".* The Word of God tells us we will be tried. We are in God's boot camp on this earth so we can expect to come up against obstacles. Obstacles and adversity should not surprise us. We know we live in an imperfect world. Whether we are living for God or not, we are going to face trouble in a world where sickness, sin, and death often prevail. God doesn't allow adversity in our lives because He wants to destroy us. He does it to prove our love and faithfulness. If we are to rule and reign with Him, we will have to prove ourselves faithful. We should not quit fighting when the battle gets hot. One meaning of the word "fiery" used in verse 12, in the original Greek text, is "calamity as a test".

Every trial and test is designed to make us stronger, not destroy us. The Bible says *"But the God of all grace, who hath called us unto his eternal glory by Christ Jesus, after that ye have suffered a while, make you perfect, stablish, strengthen, settle you"* (I Peter 5:10). God's grace will bring us through every situation if we don't turn away from Him. We cannot allow circumstances to keep us from seeking God, or exercising our faith during a trial. Trials perfect us through humility, and they should increase our awareness of how much we need God.

Although in our humanity, we will never be perfect; according to God's Word, we can be perfected. In the original Greek, the word "perfect" means to complete thoroughly repair, frame, mend, restore, prepare, and join together. Life's circumstances may have put things into our spirit that leave us broken, incomplete, or unbalanced. None of us come to God whole, or as He originally created us to be. We need God to make us whole, and allow the work of His Spirit to perfect us. This is the problem with turning from God in fear and unbelief when we get hurt by life or people.

It is in our best interest to allow God to put back together the broken pieces like the master carpenter He is. Earthly carpenters do something called framing. This is how they complete the inner structure of a building. God uses situations to frame, complete, and prepare us. Like a master carpenter, God works from the inside out. We don't always know what is inside that needs reframing, but God does. We can be sure that if we cooperate with God's process, He will do a perfect work in our lives that we will be able to testify of.

Fear Enters Paradise

The Word used in the King James Version for establish is "stablish". This means to set fast, to turn resolutely in a certain direction, to confirm, and steadfastly. Walking steadfastly through our trials will establish us in the path that leads to finding God's will for our lives. If we are steadfast, always turning to God regardless of our circumstances; our faithfulness will put us on the course He has for our lives. Our willfulness to remain faithful and steadfast, no matter what happens, will confirm our loyalty and unconditional love for God. When we are going through situations that we don't understand, we need to talk to God; we need to seek Him for direction.

King David said he remembered God when he was troubled. When he was so overwhelmed by the trials he faced that he felt he could not speak, he complained to God (see Psalm 77:3-4). The meaning for the Word "complain" used in Psalm 77, is to commune, declare, meditate, pray, speak, and talk (with). David understood the power of communion with God during a trial. Scripture informs us he had plenty of them. Some of them were self-inflicted, but many came from his enemies. David was considered by God to be a man after His own heart. Will God consider us to be men and women after His heart?

We must continue to believe that God is good and that He is the answer to life's problems. It was not God's fault if someone abused us. God did not allow it. We live in a fallen, temporal, world where sin and death have the preeminence. One day there will be a Kingdom established where righteousness will reign. God chooses not control the will of others or the foolish decisions they make. These wicked acts come from man's evil heart that does not follow God, combined with the enticement of the enemy. These things are not God's fault, but the enemy will attempt to use these things to bring us to a place of discouragement, despair, and unbelief. The devil is a liar. God has always been faithful. Even when we are unfaithful, He remains faithful and committed to His Word. Even though we may deny Him, He cannot deny Himself (see II Timothy 2:13). God does not change, even though our situations change. Trials come and go, but God remains an unchanging force in a world of confusion. He must be our source of strength.

The word "strengthen" means to confirm in spiritual knowledge and power. Handling trials God's way will give us insight into how God thinks, and cultivate the fruit of the Spirit in our lives. The ability to handle adversity will enable us to grow spiritually, and will also make us stronger. We will gain authority over the enemy because overcoming adverse situations will increase our faith. And most importantly, give us the revelation that God is a friend who sticks closer than a brother. When we know that God has brought us through a difficult time, it should be easier for us to believe He will do it again. Overcoming tribulation will empower us the next time adversity comes. We become a significant threat to the enemy when adversity doesn't stop us. Our testimony of how God saw us through our trial is a powerful weapon against the enemy.

Trials and calamities handled in the right manner will always increase our faith and the faith of others. When disasters come into our lives, they can cause us to doubt God. Doubt can allow an open door for fear to take dominion in our minds. Heart, mind, soul, and life have similar meanings in scripture. They are the will, thoughts, emotions, and life of an individual. Therefore, if fear can have dominion in our minds, it can take control of our lives. Fear takes dominion in our minds through our thinking and reasoning. We give fear an advantage in our lives when we lean on our own understanding, instead of trusting God. Our reasoning often robs us of our peace and hinders us from moving forward. We may ask questions like, why did this happen? We may begin to think along these lines: If I would have handled this another way, then this wouldn't be happening, or if I hadn't done a certain thing, a particular circumstance wouldn't exist.

And there may be some truth to this because we will reap what we sow. However, many times God will restore what the cankerworm of sin has eaten. There may be things we should have done differently, but we cannot undo the past. We accomplish nothing by focusing on past mistakes. We must learn from them, make a change for the better, and move forward. We must look to God for help, and forgive, rather than try to assign blame. We must let go of shame and regret concerning the situation. We must look ahead, focusing on what changes can be made to prevent the same thing from happening in the future. We must do away with any thoughts that are driven by fear, and the belief that we can control every situation.

When things don't go the way we think they should, we may even begin to blame God. We might think thoughts like, why did God allow this to happen? We start to question, reason and even doubt God. If we do not correct this thought process, we give fear authority instead of the Spirit of truth. The Apostle Paul had his faults, but in spite of his humanity, he did great things for God. However, his tribulations rivaled his accomplishments. II Corinthians 11:23-29 says, *"Are they ministers of Christ? (I speak as a fool) I am more; in labours more abundant, in stripes above measure, in prisons more frequent, in deaths oft. Of the Jews five times received I forty stripes save one. Thrice was I beaten with rods, once was I stoned, thrice I suffered shipwreck, a night and a day I have been in the deep; In journeyings often, in perils of waters, in perils of robbers, in perils by mine own country-men, in perils by the heathen, in perils in the city, in perils in the wilderness, in perils in the sea, in perils among false brethren; In weariness and painfulness, in watchings often, in hunger and thirst, in fastings often, in cold and nakedness. Beside those things that are without, that which cometh upon me daily, the care of all the churches. Who is weak, and I am not weak? who is offended, and I burn not?"* It appears from what he wrote that at times Paul was not only offended, but discouraged.

The word "weak", in the original Greek, literally means impotent, diseased or made feeble. Paul may have had moments when physical weakness threatened to take him off the course God had for his life. Although he was called by God, there had to be times when he felt that even God Himself was against him. After all, he had committed many prior offenses against the Church. Perhaps the thought had crossed his mind that his hardships were punishment for these things? In reality, his persecutions were a result of the great things he was accomplishing in the Spirit. However, in his humanity, he struggled. He admitted he struggled with being offended at God and man. Stating that he had to keep his conscience clear of offense on a daily basis (see Acts 24:16). He must have wondered what would happen next. The thought of giving up may have crossed his mind, but he had his hope fixed on higher things. His encounter on the road to Damascus changed his life forever.

God spoke of the things that Paul would have to suffer for His Name (see Acts 9:16). God gave Paul revelation and a vision of the higher things in Christ Jesus. His faith in God's promises was what kept him going. He knew he had to be a living example of the things he preached to others. Practicing what we preach is not always easy. Talk is cheap. Although we may know what we should do, there are times when it can be challenging to live it. This is when what we believe will be put to the test.

Paul admonished us to be disciplined in every area of our lives. He made this discipline personal, knowing if he didn't, he would be considered a castaway after preaching to others (see I Corinthians 9:27). We must follow his example. Our minds must steadfast in every situation. Isaiah 26:3 says, *"Thou wilt keep him in perfect peace, whose mind is stayed on thee: because he trusteth in thee".* The word "peace" means to be in good health, prosperity, and to be safe. When our minds are focused on God, we won't be fearful of situations, or the unknown. We will be bold, confident, and secure. We will be able to look beyond our circumstances. We will have hope for greater things, hidden things, and the mysteries of God.

God doesn't want us to know everything. He never intended for mankind to have knowledge of evil. He wants to help us and be our provider. He doesn't want us to be self sufficient. However, God does not violate our will. He wants us to have His wisdom and understanding, not the wisdom of this world. He wants us to draw near to Him. We must do this with our whole mind, soul, spirit, and then our body will obey.

Fear and unbelief are mindsets that will lead us away from God into darkness. Let's look at a definition of the word "unbelief," as it is used in scripture, according to Strong's concordance. The definition used most predominately in the Greek language throughout the New Testament is faithlessness, disbelief, and disobedience. Let's also define other variations of the word used in scripture, such as, "unbelievers and unbelieving". From these words, we get these definitions: obstinate and rebellious, to disbelieve willfully, perversely, and not obey. It is not surprising the fearful, and the unbelieving are first mentioned as those destined for the lake of fire. Revelation 21:8 tells us that the fearful and unbelieving will have their place in the lake of fire along with the abominable murderers, whoremongers, sorcerers, idolaters, and all liars.

Believing in, which includes loving and obeying God, is a willful choice that must be made every day. We must be diligent and disciplined in guarding our minds against the influence of the enemy, and this world. Most importantly, we must bring our will under subjection to the Word of God. To overcome, we must willfully clothe our thought life with humility, erasing thoughts of doubt when they first enter our minds, replacing doubt with faith. If we believe God, we will not be deceived by the enemy.

Let us go back to man's earliest interaction with God in the Garden of Eden, which occurred after the creation of the host of heaven, the earth, and all the creatures of the earth. The Bible says, *"So God created man in his own image, in the image of God created he him; male and female created he them"* (Genesis 1:27). God took the woman out of the man (see Genesis 2:21-22). It was God's plan that the first man and woman live in paradise in perfect order. God's perfect order, where peace reigned, was disturbed by sin. It was God's intention, when instituting the family, that a man should leave his parents, cleave unto his wife, and that the two become one flesh (see Genesis 2:24).

The word "cleave" used in this verse of scripture means to cling or adhere and be joined (together). God intended that man and woman should be joined s one flesh and should work together side by side together as equals in marriage. Unfortunately, in this fallen world we see an attack on marriage and the family like never before. The enemy is attempting to destroy what God had instituted from the beginning of time. The marriage between a man and woman is symbolic of our covenant relationship with God. The enemy has not only been successful at destroying the covenant of marriage and the family, but he has influenced many to break their covenant relationship with God. We must take a stand against him.

What we see happening today is not any different than what took place in the fall of man. The enemy still uses deception to get us to believe that God is somehow cheating us, and that the grass is greener on the other side of the fence. If we feel we are being deceived, all trust we have will erode. We can assume that Eve knew she could eat of any tree in the Garden, but perhaps she became dissatisfied with the provision of God, and no longer sure of what she believed. Ultimately, the Bible tells us that she was deceived.

Another meaning of the word "unbelief" is thanklessness or to be ungrateful. When a thought of thanklessness comes to our mind, we must cast it down right away. Accomplishing this can be difficult during sickness, loss, or financial trouble; but it will cause God to draw close to us in our time of crisis. Paul found peace in finding contentment in any state he found himself (see Philippians 4:11). God hates murmuring and complaining.

Scripture informs us that those who are unthankful come to a sad end. In fact, scripture says they become fools. Romans 1:21 says, *"Because that, when they knew God, they glorified him not as God, neither were thankful; but became vain in their imaginations, and their foolish heart was darkened. Professing themselves to be wise, they became fools".* The only way to overcome these "vain imaginations" is to cast them down mentally, forming or retraining correct thought processes, continuing to thank God for all He has done. Strong's outline of Biblical usage defines "vain imaginations" as a deliberating,

24

questioning about what is true, hesitation, doubting, arguing, and disputing. Unthankfulness demonstrates a lack of faith.

When we are doubtful of what we believe, circumstances will cause us to dispute and argue within ourselves. Such deliberations will prevent us from believing God for the best outcome and lead us away from God. Such was the case with Eve, who was unsure of what she believed. We might conclude that she was unsure that God wanted what was best for her. She didn't really know God or His Word, and made choices that demonstrated her lack of faithfulness. She chose to believe a lie instead of trying to find out, and learn what God said.

We must use discernment, and be aware of the source of every thought that comes into our minds. We must be sure of what we believe, standing firmly on the truth. If we begin to doubt God's Word, we can be influenced by the enemy. We have the ability to take our focus off bad things that are happening, and put our hope in the goodness of God. It is not hard to find the goodness of God. It can be found in everything, even in the air we breathe. We must let His praise continually be in our mouths. We must glorify Him in the good times and the bad.

The enemy will attempt to use the same strategies he used with mankind in the Garden of Eden. His ultimate goal is to separate us from God. Man gave the devil authority through sin, but God made a way for us to get it back. To have jurisdiction over satan, we must be under the authority of God. We cannot be under God's authority unless we are submitted to His laws. His laws are just, true, and best for us. But satan doesn't want us to believe this. Our refusal to move beyond past trauma is a device used by the enemy to paralyze us. It is a method he uses to prevent us from being who God created us to be. If he can get us to believe that we are missing out, and make the world's ways look enticing, we will fall. Should we fall, we must not fail to get back up. Too many fall, and because they think people are judging them, fail to get back in the fight.

Fear of what people think, and misguided thoughts regarding how God feels about us, will cripple us. With no power of his own, our enemy can only conquer us if he can capitalize on our bad decisions, and get us to succumb to his terror tactics by using shame and fear. If he can succeed at keeping us bound, not forgiving ourselves for our mistakes, then we are no threat to him. Another tactic he will attempt to use against us is what our flesh lusts after through covetousness. When we are worrying, focused on what we don't have, or what the world has, we will not be concerned with our relationship with God. We must be determined to focus on eternal, heavenly riches, and not be bound by the temporal things.

We can be sure that when we are struggling or vulnerable, our enemy will show up to tempt us to do what God would not have us do. We have the sword of the Spirit as our weapon. We must know and use our weapon. Scripture tells us that satan is always defeated by the Word of God. In a foolish attempt to conquer Jesus, satan tempted Him in the wilderness when He was fasting. Jesus didn't fight with satan, but conquered him by rebuking him with the Word. When satan contended with the archangel Michael over the body of Moses, Michael rebuked satan with the Word (see Jude 1:9). Scripture tells us the Word is God. Therefore, when we stand in faith upon his Word, we have God standing with us.

The Word of God is a powerful defense against the enemy for those who believe. We must know the Word in order to stand against the darkness. While we do not need to fear our enemy, we must not let our guard down, nor can we be ignorant of his devices. We must take a stand against the devil on a daily basis. The devil is becoming more aggressive because he knows his time is short, and he is doing just as the Bible said he would.

The devil uses the things of this world in an attempt to replace or cheapen the good life of living for God. While God can take a disaster, and bring something good out of it, satan will attempt to use a tragedy to destroy us. The devil is a liar and an imposter. He will attempt to present false evidence against what is actually true. It is satan's goal to deceive us, destroy our faith, bring us into fear, and to cause us to sin. He wants to make us ashamed in order to get us to backslide; hoping we will separate ourselves from God. In spite of any feelings of unworthiness due to our failures, God has counted us worthy of redemption.

Therefore, we do not need to validate ourselves to those who don't believe; the scoffers and mockers, accusers of the brethren, or even our family members. Scripture says we are the temple of the living God. We must not allow satan into our temple through thoughts of doubt, opening the door to fear, which will result in our unbelief. The mindset that we should know everything God knows, that we don't need God, or that we can be our own gods, originated when sin entered in. This mindset is the basis for humanism. We must be aware that faith in our own limited abilities is our biggest enemy.

Humanism will always be a roadblock to the miraculous. And for those who embrace this mind-set, it will cause them to be separated from God. Consider the opinion of religious humanist and minister, Kenneth Phifer. "Humanism teaches us that it is immoral to wait for God to act for us. We must act to stop the wars and the crimes and the brutality of this and future ages. We have powers of a remarkable kind. We have a high degree of freedom in choosing what we will do. Humanism tells us that whatever our philosophy of the universe may be, ultimately the responsibility for the kind of world in which we live rests with us" (Edwords 1989).

This mindset would have us put our faith in the arm of flesh, suggesting we have no need of God. This thinking had its origin in the tree that gave mankind knowledge of good and evil, where innocence was lost, and sin and death entered the world. Many blame God for everything bad that happens, and what's more: they have no fear of God. When mankind becomes their own god, there is no order. The humanistic ideology that was birthed at the fall of man has resulted in much darkness and destruction. These ideologies would have us believe we have no need of God, His Word or His commandments. This belief system also has been a leading cause of genocide, which is the total lack of respect for creation. This is a hopeless, man-made, ideology that offers no hope for redemption.

Thankfully, God has a plan of salvation, and a hope for eternal life for those who are faithful. While men fight to establish peace on the earth, it is not to be in this present age. One day there will be a tree for the healing of the nations. Until then, we must let all nations (all those who will hear) know that God is real, that He has a plan for them, and that they can be born again. We also must warn them of the subtle tactics of the enemy. We need wisdom and understanding from God, if we are to stand against the wiles of the enemy in this evil day we are living in. We must have a fresh breath of God's Spirit every day if we are to win the battle for our souls. We must start our day with prayer, giving God the first fruits of our day.

God walked with mankind in the cool of the day (see Genesis 3:8). In the physical realm, we can assume that the cool of the day would be in the morning. However, the word "cool," used in Genesis 3:8, means wind, breath, and life. When God breathed His breath into the man Adam, he became a living soul. It is the Spirit of God that gives man life, not only in a physical sense but spiritually speaking. It is our soul and spirit that are eternal. We should care for the eternal part of our being as we do our physical body. Romans 8:13 says, *"For if ye live after the flesh, ye shall die: but if ye through the Spirit do mortify the deeds of the body, ye shall live"*.

The Spirit of God enables us to live righteously, and win the fight for our salvation. If we allow our human thinking and reasoning to tell us what is right or wrong, instead of living according to God's laws, we will be led astray. We must put to death the sinful acts that seem right to our nature. God's garden only had one law. They were not supposed to eat from the tree of the knowledge of good and evil. They were warned that if they did, they would surely die. God did not lie. The day they ate of that tree they died spiritually. Sin created a breach between the Spirit of God and man. Through the plan of salvation, the Spirit of God can bring life back into man's dead spirit. The Spirit of God is the Spirit of life. Revelation 11:11 says, *"And after three days and an half the Spirit of life from God entered into them, and they stood upon their feet..."*

The Spirit of God not only gives us the power to become sons of God, but it also provides us with the strength to overcome the assault of the enemy in our lives. When the power of the Holy Ghost is at work in our lives, He can make our hopeless situations take on new life. These things then become a weapon we can use against the enemy. This is when our tragedies become a testimony to the grace of God. Without tribulation, we would have no testimony of the love and grace of God for this fallen world to see. God will turn our troubles into testimonies of His Resurrection Power.

When the devil comes to torment us with our past, and we choose to put faith in Calvary; the Spirit of God will rise up to vindicate us. God will use what the devil meant for our destruction to give us the victory. To maintain our victory, we must be walking after His Spirit, where there is no condemnation. Because of Calvary, man's sin is no longer fatal when it is repented of. Jesus has blotted out the handwriting that was against us, and has taken away the sting of death from those who keep His covenant.

It should be noted at this point that the word "man" is not gender specific when used in scripture. When we use this word pertaining to God's plan, purpose, and promises, it applies to men and women. God called both of them Adam (see Genesis 5:2). The word "Adam," and the word "man," have the same meaning in the Hebrew language. They mean mankind, either an individual or the species. God created mankind in His image for relationship, and to carry out His purpose on the earth. Only man has been given freedom of choice, and authority from God to accomplish the will of God in the earth.

The only way that man can accomplish the will of God is to become unified with God through His Spirit. The Spirit of God will reveal to us the will and mind of God. However, all revelation must be consistent with the written Word of God. In fact, the written Word of God is not only the mind of God; it is a written covenant for man to live by. We must align our thinking with God's, in order to do His will.

It has always been God's will for man to rule with Him as a son. If we are to be sons of God, then we must be led by His Spirit. Romans 8:14 says, *"For as many as are led by the Spirit*

of God, they are the sons of God". To be led by God's Spirit means
that we are sensitive and open to the will of God, and the moving
of His Spirit. God is a moving Spirit according to Genesis 1:2. We
must live by the principles of God's Word, and not by our human
emotions. The Word "Spirit" in reference to God's Spirit means
breath, mind, or disposition. God's Spirit is a life-giving force
and is the heart and mind of God. We must take on God's
attributes if we are to become sons of God. We must align our
will with His will. When we do this, He becomes a father to us,
and we become joint heirs with Christ (see Romans 8:17). That
means we inherit what He has, including eternal life. Although
we may be called to suffer, we are also called to glory. We must
choose to be lead by the Spirit of God, not the spirit of fear.

It will require consistent effort on our part to conform our
thinking to His, and overcome the mindset of the world. The
mindset of the world wants no part of sacrifice, discipline or
God's truth. Salman Rushdie, a secular humanist, made a
statement on ABC's Nightline, which gives us insight into the
mindset of all those who oppose truth. Rushdie said, "There is
an old, old conflict between the secular view of the world, and
the religious view of the world, and particularly between texts
which claim to be divinely inspired, and texts which are
imaginatively inspired. I distrust people who claim to know the
whole truth, and who seek to orchestrate the world in line with
that one truth. I think that's a very dangerous position in the
world. It needs to be challenged. It needs to be challenged
constantly in all sorts of ways" (Edwords 1989).

Take note of the word "distrust" used by Rushdie.
According to the English Thesaurus, "distrust" and "disbelieve"
are synonyms. One of the definitions for these words, according
to the Encarta Dictionary of North America, is to have no faith

in. The spirit behind humanism is fear, which is in opposition to faith. The enemy fears the One Truth of the One God. He is hard at work to get us to distrust God in any way he can. The devil will attempt to use our weaknesses and emotions, hoping to influence our thoughts, and bring us under his authority. Obeying God's laws will not always agree with our will. Life will not always be the way we want it to be. We all have our own ideas about the way things should be. Nobody wants to deny themselves, suffer, or make sacrifices when they are led by their own way of thinking. The humanist's view is that man should have control over everything, including his own destiny. God sees the future, and knows what is best for us.

The humanist gives no thought to the fact that, in reality, man cannot control his destiny. We have no control over the day we were born or the day we die. The humanist's mindset is in opposition to God. The Bible says that God is the potter, and we are merely the clay (see Jeremiah 18:4). God will attempt to correct, instruct, rebuke, and chasten those He loves (see Revelation 3:19). This is not to destroy us, but to fulfill the purpose He has for our lives.

We lose out on the plan God has for us when we choose to walk in our own ways. Our ways are not good. There are ways that seem right to a man, but the end of them is death (see Proverbs 14:12). Many shattered lives can testify of the destruction caused by foolish, willful choices. Scripture teaches that God has a plan for everyone. In Jeremiah 29:11, God says, *"For I know the thoughts that I think toward you, saith the LORD, thoughts of peace, and not of evil, to give you an expected end"*. The word "end" implies future, reward, and latter end. This means that a life that has been shattered by sin can be restored. The Bible tells us that the end of a thing is greater than its beginning (see Ecclesiastes 7:8). It is not God's desire to destroy us, but to perfect, and shape us into vessels fit for His Kingdom. It will take faith, and courage to stand against adversity, and do God's will. It can be frightening to put our destiny in someone else's hands, even if that someone is the God that created us, but faith exercised will empower us.

Since we do not know what tomorrow holds, and God does, it is in our best interest to let Him be our guiding light. We must come to a place where we realize that God is the only one we can trust with our destiny. We must make fear our enemy. We must take a stand against all enemies to our faith. We must cast doubt aside, and embrace the faith that works by love. Love is the catalyst that will enable us to exercise the faith we need to believe that God has a plan for us. Love is required for faith to grow, and perfect love casts out fear. The agape love of God is the most perfect and powerful source of love there is.

God's love is the key to overcoming fear. We need His love on a daily basis. We are continually being influenced on a subconscious level by our environment, circumstances, and people. This is why we must spend time in the presence of God. In His presence, we not only find joy, but peace. The enemy cannot abide in God's presence. When we abide in His presence, we be strengthened. It is essential in this hour to know what the Spirit of God is saying to individuals, and to the Churches. We must be in tune with God's Spirit, not only to understand what He is saying but to be obedient in our thought life.

Fear is used by the enemy to hinder our faith and must be cast out. Scripture tells us that we have not received a spirit of fear from God, but a Spirit of adoption, which enables us to recognize Him as our Heavenly Father (see Romans 8:15). We need a refreshing of our faith from the Holy Ghost every day.

33

Fear Enters Paradise

When we are connected to God, His Spirit will enable us to walk in liberty, making wise decisions, in spite of the battles we face. II Tim 1:7 says, *"For God hath not given us the spirit of fear; but of power, of love, and of a sound mind".* Fear was not evident in scripture until after the fall of man.

Before we look at the events that led up to the fall of man, let us look at satan's fall from his position in heaven. Scripture tells us satan was one of the most beautiful creatures God ever created. God created him to be a worship leader. Ezekiel 28:13-14 says, *"Thou hast been in Eden the garden of God; every precious stone was thy covering, the sardius, topaz, and the diamond, the beryl, the onyx, and the jasper, the sapphire, the emerald, and the carbuncle, and gold: the workmanship of thy tabrets and of thy pipes was prepared in thee in the day that thou wast created. Thou art the anointed cherub that covereth; and I have set thee so: thou wast upon the holy mountain of God; thou hast walked up and down in the midst of the stones of fire".*

The Bible tells us that satan was perfect in his ways when God created him, but his heart became lifted up. Ezekiel 28:17 says, *"Thine heart was lifted up because of thy beauty, thou hast corrupted thy wisdom by reason of thy brightness: I will cast thee to the ground...".* We learn that satan had attempted to pridefully exalt himself above God. The pride in satan's heart led to his rebellion towards God. Looking back to one of the literal meanings of the word "unbelief," which is rebellion, we see that satan was the first to display its characteristics. It is apparent there was no love for God in his heart or respect for God's position of authority.

Unfortunately, our thought life can be influenced by this fallen angel. We may forget that we have a position in God. There may have been times we haven't recognized or respected

His authority in our lives. There may have been times we haven't fully believed that God has the power to do what He says He will do or that He will do it for us.

We might be able to believe God will do things for others. However, poor self-image, past failures, and disappointments may hinder us from believing in the promises that God has for us. This way of thinking is a product of shame, fear, and an enemy of our faith. Shame has brought many out of covenant with God. Shame and pride work together. These are two enemies born of our fallen nature that must put under our feet. They will cause us to exalt our thoughts above the Word of God.

Pride is hated by God. If we do not cast it down, like fear, pride will result in sin, and a breach of the covenant. Pride is exalting our thinking above the mind and Word of God. This way of thinking is disobedient and humanistic. It is in our fallen nature to think and reason from a humanistic point of view. Therefore, if we are not bringing our thoughts into captivity, aligning them with the Word of God; God's power in our lives will be limited. As a result, we won't expect too much out of God or ourselves. This is a trap many fall into, becoming satisfied with the way they are. The statement "we are only human" can be dangerous to declare and live by.

It is this type of thinking that causes many to be lost in our Father's house. We all have shortcomings because of our humanity, and for this reason, we need the power of God to overcome our weaknesses. We can be sure that God will make up the difference if we are obedient to Him. An example in scripture would be the Apostle Paul, who struggled with what he called a thorn in his flesh. Although we don't know what the thorn was, we know it was a weakness in his life. The good thing about Paul's weakness, from a spiritual stand-point, is that it kept his heart from being lifted up. God's strength was perfected because of his weakness (see II Corinthians 12:9).

Fortunately, God has given mankind the power of repentance. This is something that satan does not have. The devil cannot turn to God and find forgiveness, but is forever bound to darkness. II Peter 2:4 says, *"God spared not the angels that sinned, but cast them down to hell, and delivered them into chains of darkness, to be reserved unto judgment"*. This scripture lets us know that the devil had some followers when he rebelled against God.

The devil and his cohorts have darkness attached to them until the Day of Judgment. The word "hell" literally means to incarcerate in eternal torment. It is a place to be avoided at all costs. The word "chain" means to fasten as binding or drawing. These fallen angels are prisoners as a result of their rebellion. They would have us to be like them if they could deceive us into believing that God's ways are bondage. In reality, it is the spirit of rebellion that brings us into bondage. Our enemy doesn't give advance warnings of the consequences of our actions. The word "darkness" means gloom (as shrouding like a cloud). Our enemies literally have a burial shroud surrounding them until the day God does with them as He chooses. The spirits that fight against us have to drag darkness with them, along with an impending death sentence. This explains the negativity and despair we feel when we are oppressed by the enemy, and the cohorts of his kingdom.

The word "shroud" means the dress for the dead. These fallen angels have no hope to be in the presence of God again. They are forever bound and surrounded by death and darkness. When we are tempted to make foolish decisions that lead us away from God, we should consider the value of our soul. We should also consider the consequence, and the risk we take of ending up in hell. Hell is not hell because of fire and brimstone. Hell is hell because of the absence of the presence of God.

The Bible tells us that satan was created with pipes, tabrets, and many brilliant and precious stones. The word "lucifer" means light bearer. It was satan's job to worship God and reflect His glory. He was called the anointed cherub that covereth (see Ezekiel 28:14). The word "covereth" means to protect or defend. Therefore, it was satan's job to reflect and preserve the glory of God, two positions, which he failed miserably at. Since he wanted to be above God, he could not do the will of God, because he was out of order. Therefore, his beauty lost its value. Possibly, it was at this point that satan, and an estimated two-thirds of the angels, who apparently rebelled with him, were thrown out of heaven.

Jesus said that He saw satan fall like lightning (see Luke 10:18). Jesus made this statement after His disciples came back rejoicing because devils were subject to them. Jesus reminded them, telling us as well, that we have been given ALL power to tread upon serpents and scorpions, and ALL power over the enemy. He exhorted them not to rejoice over spirits being subject to them, but to rejoice that their names were written in heaven.

We must remember that keeping our covenant with God should be more important to us than anything else. We cannot allow fear to prevent us from fulfilling the greatest commandment, regardless of nationality or culture because all commandments are fulfilled in loving our neighbor as ourself. Accomplishing these shows those outside the Church that we are the children of God. As children of God, it is now our responsibility to protect, and reflect the glory of God. This is the reason why we have an enemy. We took his position, and he is very bitter about it. Since the enemy has no forgiveness capabilities, he will stop at nothing to destroy us. He hates mankind because we are created in God's image. To be on the offensive, let's look at how our enemy operates. Then we will have a better understanding of how to overcome him.

We know that when satan was cast to the ground, his light bearing ability taken from him, and he is bound to a shroud of darkness like a man with a death sentence over his head. The devil carries death and fear with him but has no real power of his own. The devil is powerless unless God allows him to do something. Three of the main manipulative tactics he uses to assault our human emotions are fear, intimidation, and temptation. If we read what the Bible says about the condition of the earth when the Spirit of God moved upon the face of the waters, we find that the earth was "without form and void". The earth at that time was in darkness, and the Spirit of God moved upon the waters (see Genesis 1:2).

The two words "without form" have many applications in the Hebrew language, as they are used in Genesis 1:2. Some of these are: to lay in waste, desolation, confusion, empty place, wilderness, and a place of chaos. The word "void" means an indistinguishable ruin or emptiness. If we take a look at the Word "darkness," we find that the earth at that time was in terrible shape. "Darkness" in this scripture literally means destruction, death, misery, ignorance, sorrow, and wickedness. The good news is that the Spirit of God was also present, and moving on the face of the waters. The word "move" means to brood, be relaxed, or flutter. It appears from reading this scripture that the Spirit of God is drawn to darkness, destruction, and emptiness. These are things mankind rejects, but not our good God. God has the ability to fill empty vessels with righteousness, peace, and joy in the Holy Ghost.

Many people can say that at the lowest point in their lives, God was there to restore them. It is interesting to note the Word "brood" regarding the moving of the Spirit. Brooding is the protective measure a hen takes in caring for her chicks. Jesus made a statement as He wept over the city of Jerusalem. He said He wanted to gather its children under His wings as a hen does her chicks, but they would not (see Luke 13:34). It is the nature of God to restore because God is love. Love that comes from God is the most powerful force that exists. It can overcome and cover a multitude of sins. Love is stronger than death. Hatred cannot overcome love. And neither can fear.

When we realize the power of God's love, and the extent of His love, we will be the most influential people on the face of this earth. There is nothing that can compare with God's love. He stands above and beyond all that can be imagined by the human mind. He doesn't even have an opposite. However, there is a detriment to love and faith, and that is fear, which is inherent in our fallen, carnal nature, and the human emotion shame. These the enemy can work with, and very often does. But we don't have to let him. The Bible tells us that faith works or gets its energy from love (see Galatians 5:6).

Some say that fear is faith in the devil, and this may be a true statement. The devil is the king of fear, and has every reason to be afraid. After all, he has no power of his own, he is destined for the lake of fire, and he can be trampled upon by the Church. His only hope for some type of revenge is if he can get into our minds, and convince us to think like him. He is very subtle and skilled at doing this. The devil has had centuries of practice in deceiving mankind. Therefore, we cannot be ignorant of his devices, but we do not have to fear him. Proverbs 29:25 says, *"The fear of man bringeth a snare: but whoso putteth his trust in the LORD shall be safe"*. The Word of God tells us to trust in the Lord.

Our fear will cause us to fall into danger. The Word "snare" as used above, can mean a noose for an animal, or a hook for the nose. We don't have to let the enemy lead us with wrong thoughts, or the things he tries to entice us with. We can come against him with truth. Let's go back to the when the earth was without form and void. Is it possible that the earth was not that way until satan fell like lightening? While there is no scripture that says this is what happened, we do find scripture that tells us that satan was in the Garden of Eden. Ezekiel 28:13 says, *"Thou hast been in Eden the garden of God"*.

Looking back at the definitions of "form" and "void" we can deduce that is is possible something catastrophic happened that caused the earth to be in a state of ruin. If this was the case, it could mean that something was there before the destruction. Although the darkness was present upon the face of the waters, the "brooding" Spirit of God was ready; waiting to restore what had been destroyed. God is never taken by surprise. He always has a plan. When the earth was in a state of ignorance, confusion, and wickedness; God was light in the darkness.

We see an analogy to this scenario in the lives of many who come to God after a lifetime of destructive behavior. Many have had their lives seemingly destroyed by poor choices, and the oppression of the enemy. They have been bound by darkness, but God was there, waiting to receive them with open arms, in the same manner that the father responded to the prodigal son (see Luke 15:20). In spite of the destruction caused by sin, God knew that in the fullness of time, the plan He had set in motion at the foundation of the world would be fulfilled. Ephesians 1:10 says, *"That in the dispensation of the fullness of times he might gather together in one all things in Christ, both which are in heaven, and which are on earth; even in him"*.

God has a plan of escape available to anyone who wants to be delivered from sin, and the temporary, deceitful, pleasures of this world. These things only last for a short time, then leave us empty, wounded, and eventually lead to death. We must guard our souls against the mindsets of this world that are woven into the fabric of our society. For those who love God, the most dangerous mindsets are those little things we think are not that bad, the little foxes, but in reality are subtly introducing fearfulness, confusion, and complacency into our thinking.

For example, when things do not go as we had planned or prayers are not yet answered; we know it's wrong to blame God. Initially we don't, but then something else goes wrong, this triggers thoughts back to prior hurt and disappointment. We may become fearful of the next bad thing that will happen. We may even begin to dwell on the bad things that can happen, and begin to believe that they will. These things creep into our subconscious, whether we acknowledge them or not, and lead to unbelief. This is the time to pray, taking our complaints to God.

In another scenario, nothing bad has happened, but we get very busy worried about all the things that we have to do. We have well meaning people that tell us, "Don't worry, God understands how busy you are". Little by little, we spend less time praying and seeking God. It may seem that everything is okay, but suddenly the things of God become less important as we are subtly desensitized to the Spirit of God. Again, regardless of life's circumstances, our enemy knows how to use this world, and our flesh to separate us from God.

Fear Enters Paradise

We must be very careful about the things that we let influence us. Just because something sounds good doesn't mean it is. There are many things that sound good to man, but the end of these things is death. We are never warned about the outcome of our poor choices. If we were, we would live a lot differently. What may seem good to us, may be the very thing that can lead to spiritual death. In Paul's account of the thorn in his flesh, we are made aware that although he may not have liked the thorn, it was of value to his walk with God. It is evident that Paul's reaction to the thorn is what brought the power of God into his life. If Paul would have complained or walked away from God, his end would have been different. In our humanity, we may not be able to fully comprehend suffering. Most of us would be like Peter, who couldn't comprehend Calvary, but suffering is what brought salvation to all of mankind. No one in their carnal mind would want to go through suffering of any kind.

Humanism will tell us that we don't have to, and that any God who would allow us to suffer doesn't love us. The humanist doesn't consider that God is an ever present help in time of need or His goodness to all humanity. The humanist doesn't consider the value of repentance, or the consequences of our actions. Humanism will deceive us into taking matters into our own hands, and lead us down the wide path that leads to destruction. Humanism is all around us, and its mindset, which opposes God, assaults our minds every day.

In example, Robert G. Ingersoll, who is a self-proclaimed humanist, states the deception promoted by this mindset, and the false sense of freedom the enemy gives those in rebellion to God. "When I became convinced that the universe is natural, that all the ghosts and gods are myths, there entered into my brain, into my soul, into every drop of my blood the sense, the feeling, the joy of freedom. The walls of my prison crumbled and fell. The dungeon was flooded with light, and all the bolts and bars and manacles became dust. I was no longer a servant, a serf, or a slave. There was for me no master in all the wide world, not even in infinite space. I was free--free to think, to express my thoughts--free to live my own ideal, free to live for myself and those I loved, free to use all my faculties, all my senses, free to spread imagination's wings, free to investigate, to guess, dream, hope, free to judge, and determine for myself. I was free! I stood erect, fearlessly, and joyously faced all worlds" (Edwords 1989). Ingersoll's statement gives insight into the mind of someone who is deceived, and has come to the conclusion that there is no God.

He believes he is free, can make his own laws, and does not have to answer to anyone. But this is not true, and lawlessness will bring bondage, death, and destruction to all who choose it. This statement comes from a heart that is lifted up, rebellious, and disobedient. Ingersoll took satan's bait, became deceived, and believed he could become "as a god". This is the mindset of this age. It is common in our day for many not want to make commitments to anyone, or anything, other than themselves. And many do not want to feel convicted because this might make them feel they should change their behavior.

Unfortunately, this mindset can creep into the lives of Christians. It takes work, and sacrifice to do the will of God. The road isn't always easy, but neither is living without God. The path to hell is very wide. This is something we should always remember, especially when doubt, fear, and unbelief attempt to creep into our lives. We must take heed if we stand, lest we fall. Although we may come to God with good intentions; when life happens, it can be easy to be disappointed by events that come our way. If we are not prayerful, our disappointment can become a bitter root, rendering us defenseless against the enemy, allowing rebellion and disobedience to creep into our hearts.

If we allow these things to remain, the evidence of offense will eventually become evident in our behavior. We will begin to make, and live by our own rules. We may even begin to twist the Word of God to make our actions seem acceptable. Then deception, fear, and disobedience will lead us to believe that our own way is better than the way of God. This results in man elevating his ways above the laws of God. Our thoughts will never be higher than His. We must remember that a desire to know all, and be "as gods" is what led to the fall of man. This desire is inherent in the nature of all men.

Let's look at the interaction between the devil and Eve. In doing so, we can see where the ideology of humanism comes from. Genesis 3:1-5 says, *"Now the serpent was more subtle than any beast of the field which the LORD God had made. And he said unto the woman, Yea, hath God said, Ye shall not eat of every tree of the garden? And the woman said unto the serpent, we may eat of the fruit of the trees of the garden: But of the fruit of the tree which is in the midst of the garden, God hath said, Ye shall not eat of it, neither shall ye touch it, lest ye die. And the serpent said unto the woman, Ye shall not surely die: For God doth know that in the day ye eat thereof, then your eyes shall be opened, and ye shall be as gods, knowing good and evil".*

When the devil realized Eve didn't talk to God, he began to entice her with knowledge she didn't have. God never told Eve she couldn't touch the tree. According to scripture, God told Adam, before creating Eve, that if he ate from the tree, he would die. The enemy was successful at getting Eve's focus on what she didn't have, instead of all she had. Then he tempted her with the prospect of getting what she felt she didn't have without God's help. James 1:14 says, *"But every man is tempted, when he is drawn away of his own lust, and enticed"*. It is not good to spend time dwelling on what we don't have.

We should always be focused on what we do have. It is easy to become deceived when lusting after things. The desire for things has caused many to leave the faith, seeking after the vain things of this world, and to suffer much sorrow (see I Timothy 6:10). The enemy capitalized on Eve's lack of knowledge of God's Word, and the fact that Adam did not use the dominion God had given him. It would seem that what satan said sounded better to them than what God had said.

Paul warned Timothy that the time would come when men would not want to hear the truth, but would want to hear things that sounded good to their carnal mind. II Timothy 4:3 says, *"For the time will come when they will not endure sound doctrine..."*. Our carnal mind does not have the potential to love God or His truth (see Romans 8:7). In fact, our fallen, human nature quite often displays hatred towards God. It is in our nature to want to make our own laws, and follow after our own heart. When faced with the consequences of our actions, and shame sets in, instead of seeking power from God to overcome, the tendency may be to turn away from God, rather than turning towards Him. This was the case with Adam and Eve. They did not turn towards God in repentance or take responsibility for their own actions. They hid and tried to assign blame.

If we have struggles and downfalls, we must not follow after Adam and Eve's example. Scripture gives us a better example in the life of a shepherd boy who became king. David was a man after God's heart (see I Samuel 13:14 and Acts 13:22). He was a worshipper of God, and he sought after God for answers to his problems. One of the biggest problems we have as Christians is that we don't always go to God with our problems as we should. Often, we seek the advice of others, or the world's solutions, instead of praying, and seeking the face of God. We exalt our problems over His Word, and even His Name. God sees our unbelief as wickedness and disobedience. We must break the habits of self-sufficiency, and/or codependency on others to solve our problems. While we do need each other, we should not trust in the arm of flesh. We must be men and women after God's heart, and we must be about our Father's business. We need to exercise our faith during opposition by seeking God.

David's life should encourage us. He was not without sin, but God still used him. David maintained his covenant with God throughout his lifetime. He fell into sin the same way that Adam and Eve did. He was not where he was supposed to be. He was not doing what he was supposed to be doing, and he was thinking about things he should not have been thinking about. He allowed himself to become snared by the three points of sin. He looked, he lusted, and he chose to listen to the temptation of the enemy instead of obeying the laws of God (see II Samuel 11:1-4). God, in His mercy, came to deal with David concerning his sin through the prophet Nathan (see II Samuel 12:7).

Whenever God brings conviction to us, He is doing so to bring us to repentance, and a place of restoration. Although David did initially try to cover his sin, when conviction came to him, he repented (see II Samuel 12:13). David's willingness to repent saved him, and even though he had to pay a price for his sin, it did not permanently sever his covenant with God.

Such was not the case with Adam and Eve. Their sin didn't end with eating the forbidden fruit. Their disobedience resulted in fear and shame, which caused them to hide from God. When

God confronted them, they did not accept responsibility for their actions. Genesis 3:9-13 says, *"And the LORD God called unto Adam, and said unto him, Where art thou? And he said, I heard thy voice in the garden, and I was afraid, because I was naked; and I hid myself. And he said, Who told thee that thou wast naked? Hast thou eaten of the tree, whereof I commanded thee that thou shouldest not eat? And the man said, The woman whom thou gavest to be with me, she gave me of the tree, and I did eat. And the LORD God said unto the woman, What is this that thou hast done? And the woman said, The serpent beguiled me, and I did eat"*. When questioned by God, Adam blamed Eve for giving him the fruit, and God for giving him the woman. We know that Eve did not force the fruit on Adam.

Adam did not acknowledge his disobedience for eating the fruit, or for failing to take dominion over the garden. Instead he blamed God, and Eve. Adam's response was one of bitterness and rebellion. Eve didn't take responsibility either; she blamed the serpent for deceiving her. In this portion of scripture, we see the first recorded act of disobedience to the greatest commandment, which is to love God, our neighbor, and ourselves. These are bitterness, rebellion, and shame.

It is clear to us that Adam and Eve were unrepentant. They both wanted to blame someone else. This reaction was most likely motivated by fear, and is in tune with the way of the world, and modern psychology. This philosophy focuses on the past, looking for somewhere to place blame, and does not teach us to take responsibility for our actions. Many who sit in prisons today blame their childhood for what they have done. Many believe that they are the way they are because of what someone else has done. This is a very dangerous way to think. We should never encourage self-pity. We must have compassion, but self pity will do nothing but take us to the pits of hell.

Jude 22-23 says, *"And of some have compassion, making a difference. And others save with; fear, pulling them out of the fire; hating even the garment spotted by the flesh"*. While we should have compassion, being motivated by the fear of God to restore others, we should never enable them to stay in their sin or encourage self-pity. This a most dangerous mindset that has brought many Christians out of covenant with God.

This mindset is driven by fear and shame, and is a snare of the enemy. It is the scheme of the enemy to get us to come out from under the protection of God's authority. Sin will manifest itself in many ways. Sin will always beget more sin, and has no part in faith. Let's be determined to walk in faith, exercising the authority God has given us over the enemy. The first step forward is choosing to believe that God is for us, and that He loves us, no matter what our circumstances are.

Be ye mindful
always of his
covenant;
the word which
he commanded
to a thousand
generations...
1 Chronicles 16:15

Chapter Two
When Fear Strikes God's Anointed

If we are to make our covenant with God sure, we must continually exercise the measure of faith that has been given to us. Scripture tells us, *"without faith, it is impossible to please Him"*. The amount of faith we demonstrate is a reflection of our love for God. Therefore, it is the goal of our enemy, who is fear and hatred, to rob us of our faith. The enemy will attempt to discourage us through the tragedies that life brings our way. When a crisis comes, he will do his best to make a bad situation worse with thoughts of negativity, and hopelessness. Unfortunately, he has been successful in getting many to blame God for all the bad in the world. When in reality, he is ultimately the cause of all the evil in the world.

If we allow ourselves to base what we believe according to our emotions, we will not be able to discern the strategies of our enemy. If we are not diligent in our faith, we can go through life deceived and defeated. We have been given examples in scripture of those who had great faith, and those who failed to exercise their faith. The journeys of the children of Israel show us the importance of trusting God. Some hindrances to our faith are; listening to the voice of the enemy, our emotions, allowing negative thoughts to remain, and failing to replace negative thoughts with positive thoughts and thanksgiving.

We must fight against the negativity that will attempt to bring us low when we face difficult situations. This is the time to focus on and magnify the Lord. This is the approach Mary took when the angel brought her news of God's plan for her life (see Luke 1:46). Negativity will not change a bad situation, but only make it worse. We must fight back by praying in the Holy Ghost.

When we begin to have negative thoughts, we must recognize that they are not from God. We must cast them down by replacing them with positive thoughts. All negative thoughts lead to unbelief, and cause doubt in God's Word.

Once we begin to doubt God's Word, it is very easy for a stronghold of deception to form, and cause us to believe things that are not true. Doubt is the root of deception. It is important in our relationship with God, to believe that He does not have the ability to lie, and He has all power in heaven and earth. When we begin to doubt God's promises and power, we have put a limit on what He can do in our lives.

When God doesn't act because of our doubt, we can become deceived on many levels. We can form a belief that God doesn't love us, and that He will not come through for us. God acts according to our faith. An unchecked thought that began with a little doubt can escalate into a huge relational problem between God and us. Doubt was the cause of the fatal tragedies that befell the children of Israel on their way to the Promised Land.

Although they witnessed deliverance and mighty miracles, when trouble came, they doubted, and turned away from God. Because of what they chose to believe, they became deceived and fearful. They continually provoked God to anger with their stubbornness and fearfulness to their own hurt. According to Psalm 78:10, their unbelief and disobedience was a sin before God, and ultimately resulted in a broken covenant.

They allowed themselves to be motivated by fear when they faced adversity, rather than trusting God to take them to the Promised Land. They did this in spite of all the miracles they had witnessed. This remains a dilemma that God's people face today. As we know, there are many obstacles on the way to the Promised Land. Some are hindrances the enemy puts in our way. Others are placed there by God to test our faith for reasons that we can't always comprehend in our humanity. When we begin to analyze situations, our lack of understanding can cause us to doubt. The enemy observes this through our words and actions, and will attempt to manipulate our emotions with fear.

Therefore, it is important to stand on the promises of God, regardless of our current circumstance. Faith during a crisis is a sure sign to God that we love Him. It is also a sign to others that we are children of God. We must be faithful because He is faithful. God will prove us, just as He did Peter (see John 21:15-17). We cannot choose what seems to be the "easy way out" when things get rough. We must stand strong in the face of adversity. Those who are strong should strengthen the weak ones amongst us. We should continually strengthen the body of Christ. This is the will of God. We must pray continually, possessing our souls with patience. We must exercise the measure of faith God has given us so that we will be worthy to stand before Him.

Scripture teaches that every man has been given a measure of faith. Therefore, every man has some level of faith to work with. The question is, what will that measure be given over to? We need to be secure in our faith, living by deed, not just words, if we expect others to believe as we do. We must be conformed to God's image, not attempting to conform God to our image, lest we become gods in our own eyes. There is a constant danger of falling into rebellion, idolatry, and witchcraft if we do not make a conscious effort to accept some things by faith. We must always accept God at His Word. Above all things, we must be thankful. There is great peace in learning to be content in whatever situation we find ourselves in.

When we first come to God, it is easy to remain thankful. However, when difficulties arise, it is easy to become unthankful. In this "age of convenience" we live in, most do not like to face any hardship. And after entering covenant with God, many do not expect to. It is easy to become disenchanted with God and His Church. Some even become jealous and critical. We must be careful not to forget where God has brought us from. While we don't want to live in the past, we don't want to forget how we were brought out of bondage into His marvelous light. The Bible tells us that the children of Israel did not like the hardship they were experiencing on their way to the Promised Land, and wanted to go back to Egypt.

Their lack of gratitude for the liberation God had afforded them limited His ability to do the miraculous. Psalms 78:41 says, *"Yea, they turned back and tempted God, and limited the Holy One of Israel"*. The Bible says they "tempted" God. The Hebrew meaning of this word is to assay, prove, tempt, or try. Let's look into the meaning of the word "assay". This word means an analysis of something, or to examine or analyze. The children of Israel, used human reasoning, and in doing so, put human limitations on what God could do. In their analytical minds, they limited God's power. This lack of faith and unwillingness to believe that God has the best intentions for His people is similar to the mindset that brought about the fall of man. This faithlessness still troubles mankind today.

This grieves God, and may be one reason Jesus questioned if He would be able to find faith on the earth (see Luke 18:8). In the case of the children of Israel, their faithlessness caused God's wrath to fall on them. Human reasoning has caused mankind to break their covenant with God from the beginning. Before looking at the life of King Saul, let's look at the different reactions of Zacharias and Mary, concerning the promise of the Messiah. In Luke 1:11, an angel appeared to Zacharias telling him that his barren, elderly wife would have a son, who would prepare the way for the Lord, and he was to name him John. Zacharias didn't believe the promise of the angel. *"Zacharias said unto the angel, Whereby shall I know this? For I am an old man, and my wife well stricken in years" (Luke 1:18).* The word "whereby" has many applications in the original Hebrew language, but it frequently denotes opposition. Because of doubt, the Bible says Zacharias in opposition to the Word of the Lord that was spoken over his life. As a result, the angel told him he would not speak until John's birth.

How many people, who have had the call of God on their lives, react in the way that Zacharias did? He approached the fulfillment of the promise with doubt, and did not believe in God's promise. He believed according to his own intellectual capacity, only taking into consideration his own physical limitations. He did not believe God could bring the promise to pass in his life. How many have viewed themselves through their own understanding, and doubted God could ever use them or accomplish His will in their lives? We might ask, how many times have we analyzed, and limited God's ability to bring blessing into our lives?

How can we get beyond our own fears, and ways of thinking that have been a part of us for so long? It can be accomplished with a daily determination to walk by faith, regardless of what we see in the natural. We must know, and meditate on God's Word. And above all, we must live a lifestyle of prayer. Overcoming these obstacles begins with seeking God on a daily basis. Only then, will He reveal Himself to us. When we allow God to be involved in every aspect of our lives, we will come to an understanding how powerful God is. When we are in the presence of God, our enemy will flee.

Some people never come to this understanding because they shut God out with unbelief. He will not override human will. Also, if we believe in Word only, and not in deed, we limit Him. When we limit God by acting in ways that do not demonstrate faith, He cannot show us His glory or power. If we do not allow ourselves to get beyond our finite thinking, God cannot do the things in our lives that would increase our faith. It can be a detriment to our faith when our prayers are hindered because of our choices, or because our timing isn't God's timing, or when things don't go as we had hoped. It is essential to be conscious of how we chose to react to disappointment because our reaction is often an outward reflection of our view of God. How we view God can be dependent on our past experiences. When things go wrong, we must focus on God's promises, remembering the great things He has done. This helps increase our faith, and gives us the fortitude we need to see the promise come to pass. And enables us to keep our covenant with God.

The enemy would like us to forget, or at least have us minimize, the great things God has done. The enemy will try to use our thought life to hinder us, but he cannot do anything that God doesn't allow him to do. God gives us freedom of choice. The devil would like to control everything we do. If we listen and do wrong, he will come to remind us of how foolish, worthless, stupid, and wrong we are. The devil will bring to mind past failures to cast doubt on the promises of God. We must remember that the gifts of God are without repentance. This means that our purpose and plan will not be taken away as long as we always turn to God. If we choose to walk away, God cannot fulfill what He would like to accomplish in our lives. We should not listen to a lying devil.

When Fear Strikes God's Anointed

We cannot be ignorant of the devices he will attempt to use to defeat us. Most importantly, we must utilize the power of a made up mind. We must refuse to accept the enemy's negative influence in our lives any longer. We must purpose in our hearts to submit our thought life to God. Like Zacharias, who could not speak until he named the promised child John. We can hinder the promises that God has already spoken into our lives with questioning and doubt. Zacharias was given a second chance, and was able to speak of the mighty works of God. And God, who is not a respecter of persons, will do the same for us when we realize we are being motivated by fear and not faith. We must not let shame or fear keep us from what God has called us to do. God understands our humanity more than we do. He is long suffering, but He wants us to exercise our faith, which is evident by our obedience. He is a God that makes and keeps covenants (see Nehemiah 9:7-8; II Chronicles 6:14).

Mary, on the other hand, was surprised to learn that she would be the mother of the Messiah, but she did not oppose the Word of the Lord by doubting the promise given to her. Mary sought understanding from God regarding how He would fulfill the promise He had made to her. Mary asked the angel how shall this be, seeing that I have never known a man (see Luke 1:34)? By asking "how," she was saying, in what manner, in what way, or by what means this will be accomplished? She knew it would take a great miracle, but she didn't doubt that God could or would make a way to accomplish the miraculous. The angel explained to Mary how God would fulfill His promise, and she said, *"be it unto me according to your Word".*

God is not opposed to us asking Him for answers in times of great distress; we may not always get one, but a promise kept is better than an answer given. We must choose to believe that

God's faithfulness is greater than our ability to comprehend, or reason how it will be possible, or how it will happen. Impossible situations invite God to do the miraculous. Mary sought to know God, and His plan for her. She fully cooperated with God's plan in her desire to see it fulfilled.

It was a lack of faith, and lack of relationship with God that caused Israel to ask for a king. They wanted to be same as the nations around them. Samuel had faithfully judged Israel, but he was growing old. Samuel made his sons judges, but they were unrighteous and did not seek God as Samuel did. They took bribes and perverted judgment. The elders came to Samuel asking him to make them a king to rule over them (see I Samuel 8:1-5). Samuel tried to reason with them, reminding them that God was their king, but they would not listen. It seems that they had no desire to know God. Their focus was on those around them, and they had no faith in God's ability to lead them. Instead, they wanted a man to fight their wars for them.

They did not have faith that Samuel's sons could lead them as Samuel had, and it would seem they had good reason to doubt Samuel's sons. Sin will always open the door for fear. It would have been better for them to pray for God to raise up another prophet, but it is apparent that they did not consider doing this. Neither did they remember the great things God had done for them. The sin of Samuel's sons should not have cast doubt on God's ability to provide another righteous judge to lead them.

In our day, faith in God is sometimes based on what others in the Church do. When someone falls into sin, or fails us in some perceived way, all too often, we do not hold the real enemy responsible. We should bind together against the real enemy. We must pray for restoration, not judging, or believe that the Holy Ghost is less powerful than He really is. We must have faith in the power of God. We must believe in His grace. We must seek a relationship of love, not convenience with God. If we do not know God, it is not likely that we will trust Him because most people will not trust someone they don't know.

The elders of Israel had knowledge of God that was based on the law and tradition. Instead having faith that God would do right by them, they focused on the failures of those who were unrighteous. We see a similar problem in the leadership of our country today. It is time for the people of God to look beyond human failure, and pray for our nation and its leaders, as scripture commands us (see I Timothy 2:1-2). We cannot allow human failure or sin to cause us to turn away from God.

God has given every man freedom of choice. Sadly, there are some who leave the Church because they become too dependent on a relationship with the Pastor, or others in the Church, and do not form the relationship with God that they should. The first thing a new convert should do is develop a consistent prayer life, taking problems to our Pastor after we have prayed. Since Pastors are not God, they will not always be there to hold our hand, nor should they. A relationship with God may not be the initial reason we decide to attend Church, but it must become our main reason. A relationship with God is necessary for faith and growth. We cannot become so dependent on each other, that in the event someone disappoints us, we choose to walk out on God.

If unspeakable things happen. And there is no sin uncommon to man, it is not for us to judge. We must focus on God, not sin, and pray for restoration. We cannot focus on people, their shortcomings, or their sin. We must never allow sin to become our focus. We must magnify the One who can deliver, and bring the sinner to repentance. We do not have to fear sin.

We must live above sin, and take authority over it. God has given us the power to rise above the beggarly elements of this world. Again, a consistent prayer life will help us develop convictions, and revelation of how to exercise this authority. Many situations cannot be handled by human ability alone.

After Israel rejected God, putting their faith in the flesh, God told Samuel to appoint them a king, and to warn them what would happen when a king reigned over them. They were told that they would be servants. They would have to give a tenth of their resources to the king, and when they cried out to God because of these things, He would not hear them. In spite of the warnings, they still wanted a king to rule over them. They either did not believe these warnings or they were only focused on what they didn't have. Covetousness continues to be a roadblock to the path God would have us take. Coveting what we don't have leads to much discontentment, resentment, and in reality is sin. If it is in our heart to covet the best gifts for what God has called us to do; we will be at peace with ourselves, and with God.

The most important thing for every one of us should be our covenant relationship with God. Therefore, all other things should be considered secondary and counted as wood, hay, and stubble. Making decisions that don't involve God will bring us into bondage to shame and fear when we are left to deal with the consequences of our bad decisions. The children of Israel lost the liberty they had when they made the decision that God should be replaced with a man as their leader. We see the trickle down effect of this wrong decision to this day. God knew that giving the children of Israel a king to rule over them would not be in their best interest, but He gave them their way.

We must be careful not to make the same mistake. When we continually ask for something that is not best for us, there may be times that God will relent, and give us our way. However, in the long run, we are better off if He closes the door to what ultimately will be a detriment to us. We must have an understanding of the importance of being under God's authority. If we are not under God's authority, we will be under satan's. Providing we believe in eternity, and that the Word of God is the final authority in all things, we know that there are two eternal destinations. These are heaven, and hell.

The physical realm which we live in is not eternal. The subjects of all kingdoms are required to live by kingdom laws. Samuel was a Pastor in typology to the children of Israel. Samuel was appointed by God, and he heard from God on a regular basis. God placed a prophet over Israel to teach them, and lead them in His ways. God has not changed. We shouldn't become codependent on others, but we must be willing to receive godly counsel. When the man of God gives us godly advice, or makes decisions we might not agree with, we must act in accordance with the Word of God. If we are using our human reasoning, there is a good chance we will be wrong.

Since God has placed Pastors over us in a place of authority, we can be sure that God speaks to them. Providing we trust our Pastors, and believe that God speaks to them, we can be sure that their counsel is true. If we remain unsure, it is best to trust God, and leave it at the altar. We should pray for God to speak to our leaders because they need direction just as we do. We must keep in mind that they have a calling from God, and we will only be judged by how we act. We are only responsible for our actions. If we do not believe that our Pastor hears from God, we have a problem, and may very well end up as King Saul, who is counted among the fearful and the unbelieving.

When Fear Strikes God's Anointed

King Saul was a fearful and disobedient man. Saul's actions, and the choices he made, demonstrated his unbelief. From the time that Samuel anointed Saul king, he tried to give Saul godly counsel. But Saul continually acted outside of the counsel he was given. Samuel was there to help Saul hear the Word of the Lord, and give him direction for leading God's people. This was a concept that Saul never understood. Saul was not in tune with the heart or mind of God. Saul did not base his thinking or actions in accordance with God's Word. Saul's fears, which were never dealt with, caused him to lose the kingdom, and eventually his life.

It doesn't matter what God has called us to be if we don't get beyond ourselves, our fears, and our past. When Saul sought out Samuel regarding his father's asses, Samuel told him something beyond what he wanted to hear. It was something that was beyond his comprehension. The word Samuel gave Saul should have made him feel honored, but the account we read does not lead us to believe this was so.

Could it be that Saul felt shame concerning the actions of evil men, who slew a man's concubine, while the man and his concubine were traveling through the country of Benjamin? The Bible tells us that the men of the tribe of Benjamin refused to hand over the men responsible. These men were living within their borders. This caused the children of Israel to go to battle against their brethren, which resulted in Benjamin being the smallest of all the tribes of Israel (see Judges, chapters 19-21). This was apparently a cause of reproach for Saul.

When Saul answered Samuel, regarding his call to the Kingdom, the first thing he said was, *"Am not I a Benjamite, of the smallest of the tribes of Israel, and my family the least of all the families of the tribe of Benjamin"* wherefore then speakest *thou so to me" (I Sam 9:21)?* By asking "wherefore," Saul was saying, for what good, purpose, or reason are you asking me to be king? Could he have been saying, don't you know what kind of family I come from? Don't you know that I have a tainted past? How can you expect me to be king, and lead these people? Saul's reaction tells us that he really didn't want the position.

Saul being anointed as king is an example of God's willingness to overlook our past. This should encourage us to move forward, knowing God will give us the victory. We must not allow ourselves to be bound to the past by shame and fear. We must continually remind ourselves that the perfect work of Calvary took care of all that. When we are in blood covenant with Jesus, we can do what He has called us to do. We must walk in faith, not in fear. We cannot allow flesh or shame to hinder us.

We must conquer our human pride with humility and thanksgiving. With humility, we understand that we are called according to His purpose. We can overcome by the Blood of the Lamb, and by our testimony of how God helped us overcome. Our past failures are often the very thing God will use to save someone else. Without our testimony of overcoming our past, we cannot accomplish His will. God is not willing that any should perish. We must overcome the things of this world. We cannot allow the presence of fear (a spirit God did not give), and shame or pride (human emotions), to control our thoughts or actions. Both of these lead to unbelief and disobedience.

This iniquity contributed to Saul's downfall, and were evident in his life until the kingdom was given to David. Saul's past insecurities affected his future. Saul's actions seemed to say that he didn't take what Samuel said to heart. After Samuel anointed him, as king of Israel, the Spirit of the Lord came upon

Saul, he prophesied, and God promised to give him a new heart. These things didn't seem to change Saul.

You would think he would have been excited about these monumental occurrences in his life and would have gone home and told his family. However, when Saul returned home, and his uncle questioned him about his visit with Samuel, he didn't seem excited about being anointed king. Saul told him that the asses had been found, but he didn't tell him about the kingdom or anything else that took place that day (see I Samuel 10:16). Saul apparently did not want to tell anyone of his encounter with God. Instead of telling what God did for him, or letting others know about God's power, he kept it to himself. This was in part because he never had his own relationship with God.

If a relationship is not cultivated on a daily basis through prayer and devotional time, His power will not be manifested in our lives. We must keep in mind that receiving the Holy Ghost will not automatically change us. The Spirit of truth will lead us to all truth, but we must be willing to follow. We must embrace a relationship with God, and be willing to share Him with others. If we are fearful of rejection, and of what others might think, we will keep our relationship with God to ourselves.

The power and anointing of God are what is needed to reach a lost and dying world. It is vital for every member of the Church to manifest God's power in their lives. God's Church must prevail over the fear and intimidation of the enemy. We must proclaim the power of the blood of Jesus, rejoicing in the victory we have over our carnality, and the shame caused by past sin and failures. There must be a revival of apostolic power and authority in the perilous times we are living in. The Church must arise, and shake off the beggarly elements of this world. We must cast aside our personal problems that won't matter in eternity, making time for God's eternal kingdom. We must continue steadfastly in the apostle's doctrine to the end that we will reach the world that Jesus died for. We will not accomplish the will of God, or reach the lost if we listen to the voice of fear.

We can conclude that Saul was motivated by fear. Although he was taller than all the other people, when he was to be presented before them, he hid among the stuff (see I Samuel 10:22). On what should have been the most significant day of Saul's life, he ran and hid. Was it a fear of responsibility, or was it fear of the people? Perhaps he was afraid he would be required to change some things about himself to accomplish the task set before him. Saul was not left alone in the endeavor set before him. God laid it upon the hearts of certain men to assist Saul, but of course, there were those who spoke evil against him. There will always be someone to discourage or speak against what they don't understand. Although Saul said nothing at the time, Saul let what people thought to contribute to his downfall. As Christians, we must come to a place where we are more concerned with what God thinks than what people think. The world we live in will not always applaud us for doing what is right. Or appreciate the conviction they feel.

There are those who will, subconsciously perhaps, attempt to alter God's purpose for our lives. If we listen to those who are not on the right path themselves, we won't be walking after the Spirit. Nor will we go in the right direction. The Word of God must be a lamp unto our feet, and a light unto our paths. Especially during the worst trials of our lives. When doubt has us feeling the narrow path is the wrong one to take, we must choose to believe that God's ways are always best.

Saul did not live by God's Word, nor did he wait on God. Instead, he was motivated by his emotions and fear, which resulted in him taking matters into his own hands. Saul's lack of faith in God led to his disobedience. Saul did not trust God in the heat of the battle. Saul put more faith in the people, who fled from the Philistines, than in God.

We learn in I Samuel, chapter 13, that when the Philistines were gathering to go to war against Israel, some of the people followed Saul in fear and anxiety, others scattered from Saul, hiding in caves and thickets (see I Samuel 13:6-7). Saul waited for Samuel, but when he didn't show up, Saul did as we sometimes have a tendency to do. He took matters into his own hands instead of waiting on God (see I Samuel 13:9-12). He did not trust God to come through for him. Instead, Saul thought he could overrule what God said, and do what he thought was right. Giving in to fear lead to his unrighteousness. Saul chose to make his own rules, and do things according to his plan.

Sometimes it is not easy to wait on God. But impatience, which always results in bad decisions, can cause us to miss out on the will of God. Taking matters into our own hands shows God that we don't believe He will come through for us. God's timing is not always ours. Since God lives in eternity, seeing the end of things, He really does know what is best.

Our dilemma worsens when we begin to doubt Him; failing to believe He has our best interest in mind. We will be motivated by fear when we entertain thoughts of doubt. We can have doubtful thoughts about many of life's problems. The best way to overcome is to focus on God's Word, think about His promises, wait, and pray. When we spend time in God's presence, we will find the peace we need. If we follow our own heart, we will try to force God's hand, which never results in His best for us.

Consider the example of Abraham and Ishmael. We see fear at work in Sarah's decision to make God's promise happen.

She did not have faith that she would ever bear the promised child. Ishmael was not the child of promise; he was a child of the flesh (see Galatians 4:23). In other words, he was a product of Abraham and Sarah's will, not God's.

We learn that God will sometimes work through our mess because He is good, but we will not get God's best from trying to create our own destiny. Although God still used Ishmael to build a nation, the child of the flesh was at enmity with the child of promise and mocked him. Our plans are most often not aligned with the will of God. The carnal mind is enmity towards God. Our old man, born of our fallen nature, is our deadliest enemy.

Obedience is more important to God than sacrifice. We can wear ourselves out doing things that are not God's will. This can even involve Church duties. If we are worried we are not doing enough to please God or people, we might be motivated by fear instead of a desire to be in the will of God. God wants us to have balance in our lives. There is a perfect will of God, but it takes a lifetime of following Him to accomplish it. Following God requires continual obedience to His Word. We must have a heart after God, His Kingdom, and know His purpose.

Saul did not have a heart after God or a desire to fulfill God's will. Saul was motivated by flesh and fear. When he saw the people were scattered from him, he offered a sacrifice. According to the Law of Moses, the sacrifice Saul offered was only to be offered by a priest. It was at that time that Samuel told him that the Kingdom would be taken from him, and given to a man after God's heart. At this point, some kind of response from Saul would be expected. We would think that he would have shown repentance or some concern when he heard the Word of the Lord from Samuel, but he did not. It seems that Saul didn't take Samuel seriously. He just went about his business and gathered more men to go to battle. Samuel was Saul's spiritual leader. Saul should have received Samuel's counsel, but Samuel's counsel did not line up with how Saul felt or what was going on in Saul's life at the time.

Saul's actions are analogous to those who will not receive godly counsel or wait on God. If we do not want to receive counsel from our Pastor, it is likely because we don't believe that he is speaking in our best interest. As long as our Pastor's counsel lines up with God's Word, we should take it to heart. Decisions that go against Biblical counsel will leave us deluded, deceived, and bring us out of God's will. Those who are seeking God, through His Word and prayer, typically do not have problems receiving godly counsel.

Our greatest defense is to know the Word of God. It is a defense mechanism that enables us to measure all incoming influences to determine whether or not they are grounded in the Word. Our greatest enemy is not satan. It is self or selfishness. Self-centeredness comes from our flesh (carnal mind) and hinders our faith. Our carnal mind is easily motivated by fear due to an innate flight or fight response in our fallen nature. If we are motivated by faith, we will not feel the need to further ourselves or provide our own means. We will depend on God for everything. We will be meek (dependent on God). Those who are meek do not worry about worldly things. Those who believe that God will provide their every need, live a life of truth, righteousness, peace, and joy.

As saints of God, we must be sure what manner of spirit we are. Where do our loyalties lie? Are we a Saul or a David? From everything written, we learn that Saul did not have a love for the Kingdom or the things of God. He was motivated by his own desires and will, and led by fear and jealousy.

When Fear Strikes God's Anointed

The Bible tells us we are led astray of our own lust, and then enticed (see James 1:14). The problem begins with us. Many voices in the world will tell us exactly what we want to hear, be they human or demonic. If these voices are telling us something that is not in agreement with God's Word, we must not listen. We must replace every disobedient thought by replacing it with God's righteous Word. God's Word is our greatest weapon against disobedience. Also included are prayer, fasting, repentance, and more prayer.

Saul never repented of his disobedience or attempted to make things right with God. We know this because in I Samuel chapter 15, when Saul was given another chance to do the will of God, he once again took matters into his own hands. He was instructed to destroy Amalek, who troubled the children of Israel when they came out of Egypt. Here was Saul's opportunity to demonstrate his faith by obedience, and take vengeance on the enemy of his people. Saul did not entirely destroy Amalek; instead, he coveted the spoil. Looking at this illustration from a spiritual sense, we see the danger of unbelief and covetousness. Saul claimed he was doing the right thing when he disobeyed God by keeping the best of the spoil, but this was Saul's will, not God's. Saul went directly against the commandment of God.

I Samuel chapter 15:24 says, *"And Saul said unto Samuel, I have sinned: for I have transgressed the commandment of the LORD, and thy words: because I feared the people, and obeyed their voice"*. We have to wonder if things wouldn't have gone differently for Saul if he had been genuinely repentant. Genuine repentance closes the door on the enemy. We are not under God's authority when we are unrepentant. Instead, we fall under satan's authority. Saul could not bring himself to admit he was wrong in front of the people. His unwillingness to admit he was wrong was indicative of his spiritual condition. If we feel the need to assign blame, and can't take responsibility for our own actions, we are in trouble.

When we are unwilling to humble ourselves, turning towards God in repentance, we are placing ourselves under satan's authority. We must remember that all sin is common to man, we will never be free of sin while we are in this flesh. That is why we need to die daily to our will. If we are not steadfast in prayer, sometimes fasting, we will not be able to follow the leading of the Holy Ghost. Without devotion, prayer, and fasting, we are carnal, and it is easy to listen to the voice of the enemy.

The enemy does not want us to take responsibility for our actions because when we confess our sins, we will we be forgiven, which is something he cannot be. The enemy does not want us to change for the better; he wants us under his influence. If we sin, we should run to God, not turn away from God, which leads to more sin. We must not let shame and fear motivate us. Ultimately, it was shame and fear that brought Saul out from under the safety of God's authority. After he blamed the people, whom he had been placed in authority over, while having previously blamed Samuel for not getting there in time, he once again disobeyed the commandment of God.

Saul's failure to take responsibility for his actions, and obey God's Word, caused God to repent of making him king. His fear and shame became a snare to him. Proverbs 29:25 says, *"The fear of man bringeth a snare: but whoso putteth his trust in the LORD shall be safe"*. It is common for those who step out of the will of God, where deception has free reign, to blame the Church, and the man of God.

Again, the inability to take responsibility for our actions is a very dangerous place to be spiritually, and it will lead to spiritual death. An unrepentant heart is full of disobedience, and demonstrates a lack of faith in God. It appears from the accounts recorded regarding Saul that he was more fearful of the elders of the people than he was of God. It may be that he felt the need to exalt himself in front of the people because of where he came from, and how he felt about himself. It would seem that Saul's past hindered him from the time he was told he would be king, until the day he lost the kingdom to David. His actions indicated that he did not trust God. Saul did not know God at all. Saul was fearful, even though God chose him to be king over His people. What would have happened if Saul repented, and made up his mind to follow God's laws? It would seem that because of shame, Saul was a victim of self.

God spoke through the prophet Joel saying that His people would never be ashamed. It is not the will of God for His people to live in shame, but God won't force His grace or forgiveness on anyone. We must face fear with faith that works by love. We can't be concerned with what others think, as long as we know that God approves of us. We shouldn't worry about the rest. We can be encouraged by the promise that if we submit ourselves under the mighty hand of God, He will exalt us in due time.

God must be exalted because He is God, and worship must be pure from a heart that loves and trusts Him. When Saul was told that the kingdom would be taken from him, he begged Samuel to return again with him, and honor him before the elders and the people of Israel so that he could worship the Lord (see I Samuel 15:30). Saul's worship was not from a sincere heart. Saul said, *"honor me so that I can worship the Lord thy God"*. Again, Saul never developed a relationship with God. He did not call Him the Lord my God. He was Samuel's God, not

Saul's. Saul never got personal with God. Saul was more worried about the accolades of men than his relationship with God.

Saul was so worried about what others thought of him, he forgot to worry about the judgment of God. The enemy wants us to be crippled by fear of man; he also wants us to fear making our commitment to God sure so we will do the opposite of what God's law says. Jesus says something different, *"fear not them which kill the body, but are not able to kill the soul: but rather fear him which is able to destroy both soul and body in hell"* *(Matthew 10:28).* Saul was more worried about the loss of his earthly position than the welfare of the kingdom. Saul was not kingdom minded. He did not understand the concept of spiritual authority. Saul's inability to understand these important aspects of a relationship with God caused his downfall. If we allow ourselves to fall into the same line of thinking, it will cost us the kingdom as well. We must not allow the fear of man, or anything else, to separate us from God.

Let's look at the similarities between Saul's position with God, and ours. Saul was appointed the king, and we are made kings and priests under the new covenant with His blood (see Revelation 1:6; I Peter 2:9). Saul had someone who was appointed by God to teach him. Samuel was someone he was supposed to be accountable to. God has given us Pastors after His own heart to teach us, and lead us in the way we are supposed to go (see Jeremiah 3:15). If we aren't consistently following God's Spirit and righteousness, we become carnal, and the result is disorder. A problem occurs first in the spiritual realm, then shows up in the natural, which lets us know we are out of order. Scripture admonishes us that we don't wrestle against flesh and blood. Our battle is not with people, but with the spirits behind what they are doing. The only flesh we have to wrestle with is our own. But there are spiritual things we must fight against. These are the principalities, powers of the kingdom of darkness, and spiritual wickedness (see Ephesians 6:12). These are the things we must be aware of because if we are not, we will blame people and circumstances for everything that is going wrong in our lives.

We must come to a place of obedience and meekness, where we are entirely dependent on God. The first step is a determination to believe that regardless of what is going on, if we are walking in the Spirit, that situation will have the best outcome in the end. This is true faith and obedience. When we are disobedient to God, and those who God has placed in authority over us, the enemy sees this. We have just removed ourselves from under the protection of God's authority, and placed ourselves under the authority of another kingdom. The enemy understands spiritual authority.

He also understands the power of the Word of God. Although he doesn't respect the laws of God's Kingdom, the devil has an understanding of the power of Spiritual authority. There are hierarchies of demons under satan's authority. They hinder the righteous, and entice the willing according to their own lusts. We cannot take authority over the enemy when we are not in obedience to the mind of Christ (see II Corinthians 10:6). Our obedience puts us in a position to take revenge on disobedience. We cannot retaliate against the enemy when we are disobedient. Therefore, when we are disobedient, we become bound spiritually, and cannot take authority over wickedness because we are not in opposition to it.

Imagine an army whose soldiers do whatever they want or fraternize with the enemy. How far do you think they will go in a war? Obviously, if they go where they aren't supposed to go, and do what they haven't been commanded to do, they will end up wounded or dead. It is the same in this battle for our souls. When we are disobedient, it affects us spiritually because we have opened a door for further attack and deception. This will be evident when our actions reveal our spiritual condition.

When satan observes our disobedience, he knows he can have a foothold because shame and fear will cause us to justify our actions. If we allow sin to work in our lives, it will be accompanied by shame and fear, which will cause us to turn away from God and His people. We must not allow these evil elements to cause us to lose the battle for our souls.

We must also consider the souls of those who are watching us. We must think of our children, family members, and those whom God wants us to be a witness to. We are supposed to be a light in a dark world. We shouldn't react fearfully when something does not go right. We should stand firm in our faith, and be the ones to encourage others with prayer.

The enemy knows how to work very subtly. It is evident to us when someone commits a sin that most would consider immoral. However, even when we are not committing immoral acts, our carnal nature must be continually put under subjection. If we are not diligent in this, we can be enticed into doing things that are not of faith, which is sin, or sins of omission (see James 4:17). Saul thought he was doing the right thing when he kept the choice cattle to sacrifice, but he failed to do what God told him to do. We might think we are doing the right thing when we allow our emotions to rule our actions instead of following principles. We cannot put more faith in how we feel than in God's principals. If things don't make sense, we must choose to belief, resisting unbelief.

When Fear Strikes God's Anointed

Disobedience to the authority of God's Word will open the door for doubt, fear, and unbelief to influence the way we think. We cannot allow ourselves to become focused on circumstances or the actions of people. If we base what we are going to do on the actions of others, we are putting our faith in people. We must put our faith in God. We must realize that even if those we have depended on are failing us, God will not. We must be willing to look beyond frail humanity, and wait for the power of God to work in all situations.

Patience is a fruit of the Spirit, and it is not inherent in our nature. It is a discipline that requires much faith. We must cast all doubt aside along with our insecurities. Fear and insecurity will keep us from fulfilling the conditions of God's covenant. We cannot be man-pleasers. We must be God-pleasers, and put all of our faith in Him. Our choices, when made without prayerful consideration, typically do not have a good outcome; especially when they go against the Word of God. We must stand against the popular opinion of man, and not let our actions separate us from God. As it was with Saul, disobedience will cause our downfall. We cannot base our decisions on what people expect of us or what they think. God wants obedience from us more than anything else, *"For rebellion is as the sin of witchcraft, and stubbornness is as iniquity and idolatry"* (I Samuel 15:22-23).

Rebellion in the Hebrew text, as it is applied in this scripture, means bitterness. Saul must have embraced many things from his past. His actions reflected his bitterness, and lack of faith in God's Word, and ultimately God's love for him. It would seem that how Saul felt about himself ultimately affected his actions towards God, and those around him. Saul did not trust God to do right by him. So if things didn't make sense, he was afraid to do what God said. It appears he did not believe God

73

loved him or would come through for him. Faith and love are inseparable, and love always believes the best.

It seems that self-will, and what others thought, were more important to him than obeying God. Self-will became an idol to Saul because it took precedence over the commandments of God. Samuel informed Saul that God had rejected him as king. The Word "rejected" means to despise, cast away, and abhor. Disobedience brought Saul out of covenant with God. Unlike David, who was a lover of God, no scripture text allows us to believe that Saul loved or sought after God on a personal level.

Scripture tells us that David was aware he needed God more than God needed him. David got his strength from God, and his relationship with God made him victorious in battle. David was not a perfect man, but he was not fearful or cowardly. He loved God and His Word. What made God take notice of David was the condition of his heart. David knew the power of repentance, and he had a repentant heart. He was also a man of great faith. David was a man who had the faith to take on a giant single-handedly. David was the kind of man God was looking for to place on the throne of Israel forever.

God told Samuel to quit mourning Saul, and anoint David king of Israel. Saul continued to follow his own heart and shame based mentality. Saul's carnal mind became a stumbling block to him. There is a lesson to be learned from the life of Saul. We don't have to allow shame and fear to govern our actions. We must seek God when we fall. This is the way toward restoration. We cannot allow fear, or shame to prevent the restoration process. God is our help in time of need. Without Him, we sink further into carnality. We must keep moving forward, avoiding the quicksand that has kept so many stuck in the past.

When Fear Strikes God's Anointed

Saul would not move beyond his past or present sin. He became more bitter as time went on. When David conquered the giant Goliath, Saul became jealous after hearing the women sing about David's tens of thousands, while only attributing to him thousands. This became an obsession to Saul. He knew that David was going to take the kingdom from him and that the people were already looking towards David. The Bible says that Saul envied David from that day forward. When Saul knew that the Lord was with David, and he behaved wisely; he became afraid of David (see I Samuel 18 14-15).

Saul's fear was his downfall from the day that he entered the kingdom until the day it was taken from him. We must be aware of the effect of fear on our personal lives. We can learn from mistakes that Saul made. We have been given power, and the ability to walk in the ways of God. It is for our benefit that God has devoted so many chapters in the Bible to the life of Saul. Many valuable lessons are to be learned from scripture about the harmful effects of fear.

We can be sure that fear will lead into the sin of one kind or another. Whatever is not of faith is sin (see Romans 14:23). Jesus says that every branch that bears no fruit will be cast by men into the fire. If we are to bear the peaceable fruit of love for the kingdom, we must continually put fear under our feet. We cannot allow fear to prevent us from stepping out in faith. We must believe in the promises of God with a determination to see them come to pass. When we are determined to see God's promises come to pass, our faith will overcome the negative influences of fear. Saul never allowed the love of God to be made manifest in his life.

Saul's fear led to the attempted murder of David. Saul pursued after David until he was mortally wounded in battle.

Then he committed suicide because of his fear of the enemy. His hatred for his brother resulted in God's ears being closed to his prayers. I John 3:15 says that whoever hates his brother is a murderer, and does not have eternal life dwelling in them. Saul's jealousy and hatred eventually led to his death. When God would not hear him, he consulted a witch (see I Samuel 28:7). Unfortunately, Saul never found a place of repentance or chose to exercise his measure of God given faith.

David, on the other hand, sought after God even when the people wanted to stone him over the burning of Ziklag (see I Samuel 30:6). The Bible says that David encouraged himself in the Lord. The Word "encouraged" has many applications in Hebrew. A few of those are: be sure, behave self valiantly, and withstand. David was not a fearful man. He was a man of war, and that is what God is looking for.

He needs men and women in this hour to complete His work on this earth. Men and women who are not afraid to stand up and fight for what is right, and speak the Word of God with boldness. Are we Kingdom minded? Are we lovers of self or lovers of God? Where do we stand in our covenant agreement with God? Are we a Saul or a David? These are things we must ask ourselves when we consider our place in His kingdom; keeping in mind that there are conditions to God's covenant.

Chapter Three
The Conditions of the Covenant

A covenant is a legally binding agreement between two parties. The covenant that we enter into with God has been sealed with the blood of a spotless lamb. In our dispensation, we enter this covenant through a circumcision of the heart, not the flesh. It is our responsibility to make the effort to learn what we need to do to keep our part of the agreement, and we can be assured that God will do His part. It is to our advantage to be in agreement with God, who is the creator of covenant relationships. God has established covenant relationships with humanity because He wants a relationship with us. When we walk in agreement with God, we will have abundant life. It has always been God's desire to walk with mankind. However, in spite of God's merciful efforts towards undeserving mankind, we do not always choose to walk in God's ways. The Word of God tells us that from the creation of man to the restoration of all things, there are conditions to God's covenant. It is impossible to meet these conditions if we do not pray, know, and live according to the Word of God.

This statement is not new, but we need to be reminded, in this day of technology, that we MUST make time to talk to God, and read His Word. With all that is going on in our world, men's hearts are gripped with fear. Some blame God for the evil, but God did not give the enemy authority in this world. Mankind gave satan authority. It was a breach of the covenant that made satan the prince of the power of the air. Adam allowed death to enter, giving the enemy dominion, by violating God's covenant.

The Conditions of The Covenant

Through the rebellion and deception of Adam and Eve, sin entered the world. Then their offspring inherited their fallen nature. This fallen nature has manifested itself in many ways. In some as a mindset revolving around self, willfully walking in ways that are not God's. In others a resolve to restore what was lost at the fall of man, but not in the way that God intended. If we are going to do things that are "good," but not what God has asked, we may as well do nothing at all. Many today live for God in ways that scripture does not mention or command. Cain did not want to offer the sacrifice God required. We can conclude that animal sacrifice was required after the fall of man.

Although it isn't plainly recorded in scripture, we know that animals had to die in order to clothe Adam and Eve. We also see that the blood of the precious Lamb of God, which brought about the New Covenant, replaced animal sacrifice. God Himself chose to become our sacrifice. We know the blood of animals was required until God provided us with something better than "Abel's sacrifice". It took the precious blood of the Lamb to redeem us, and provide a way to restore the breech sin created.

Hebrews 9:12 says, *"Neither by the blood of goats and calves, but by his own blood he entered in once into the holy place, having obtained eternal redemption for us"*. Jesus is the mediator of the new covenant. The Bible tells us that Calvary declares to us a better way, with an everlasting covenant, which declares to us a more perfect sacrifice than that provided by Abel (see Hebrews 12:24). In Abel's dispensation, his sacrifice was acceptable, but it would not be today. Cain did not provide an acceptable sacrifice in his dispensation. Cain was like some today who choose to leave out the obvious commandments given by God. He had another way of sacrifice in mind.

The Conditions of The Covenant

Cain would have known that he was supposed to offer an animal sacrifice. When his sacrifice wasn't accepted, he became bitter, rebellious, and jealous of his brother. He hated the righteous acts of his brother. Cain would not be brought to repentance, or observe the requirements of God. He kept on going in his rebellious, sinful way, moving farther away from God until he slew his brother. God had warned him that sin waited at the door, and he would have to take authority over it, or it would rule him. However, Cain would not listen to God. Cain did not have a repentant heart or a teachable spirit.

God tried to counsel Cain to bring him to repentance, but Cain turned his back on God. Genesis 4:6-7 says, *"And the LORD said unto Cain, Why art thou wroth? and why is thy countenance fallen? If thou doest well, shalt thou not be accepted? and if thou doest not well, sin lieth at the door..."*. From the very beginning God made it clear that if His commandments were obeyed, Cain would be accepted. And if they were not, Cain would fall under the influence of sin. God let Cain know that he was required to observe the laws that God had set before him.

The laws God has instituted for His people have always required faithfulness on the part of both parties, not on God alone. God's covenant relationship with mankind can be compared to marriage in a spiritual sense. Marriage requires mutual respect on the part of both parties. Marriage should not be entered into with an expectation of what we can get out of it, but what we can put into it. God is not required to fulfill His promises to us without any effort on our part. We must use every available resource He has given us to accomplish our end of the agreement. God's covenant with man has stipulations of obedience and faithfulness. Love is directly relational to both faithfulness and obedience. Without love, these will be impossible to accomplish. We cannot say we love God if we do not obey His Word.

And we cannot obey what we don't know. If we do not take the time to get to know God through His Word and prayer, it is impossible to fulfill our part of the covenant. Our covenant with God is established the day we are baptized in His name. It is a blood covenant that was paid for with a great price. Salvation may be free, but it is not without a price. It will cost something to be in covenant with God. We need to count that cost, but not with the fear of this world. Not like the man who fearfully buried his only talent, knowing that God is more faithful than we are.

Whatever we give up in this world, we will be given more. We cannot expect to reap all the benefits of a relationship with God, if we do not know Him. Our part is clearly stated in our marriage agreement; the Holy Bible. If we observe and obey the laws of God, He will bless us, if not we will bring a curse on our lives. As with any relationship, our motives towards God should be righteous. Wrong motives are why many marriages don't work. People are often looking for someone to fill a void in their life or fulfill some other need. When two people think like this, it does not work. In like manner, our relationship with God requires pure motives.

Scripture admonishes us to present our bodies as a living sacrifice. This is for our benefit. If everyone stayed in the will God had for them; what a different place the world would be. God will require us to give up things that are detrimental to our eternal well-being, even if we deem them important. However, God will add more than He will ever take away. The things He wants to remove are things that we think we need, but in the long run are hindrances to the plan He has for us. God sees the future we cannot see. Those who are wise let God be in charge of

80

their lives. When we are asked to present ourselves as living sacrifices, God is saying; give your life to me so I can direct your paths, and give you the best life possible.

Many can testify to the fact that the things they gave up were later replaced with something so much better. Nothing we give up will be more than what God will give us in return. Entering into a covenant relationship with God requires sacrificing our will on a daily basis, no matter how good we think our plans are. If we are to remain in covenant with God, we must enter in with the understanding that commitment is required, even when we are going through trials, disappointments, or loss.

In an earthly marriage covenant, we can be disappointed at one time or another. At times, we may feel disappointed when we are doing our best to live righteously and things go wrong. The enemy will do his best to make us weary in well doing. It is his goal to wear out the saints of God (see Daniel 7:25). He will try to make us believe God doesn't care or isn't doing anything for us. When in reality, God has done everything for us. He will never fail or disappoint us. He will always give us His best in every circumstance we include Him in.

When things aren't going our way, we must keep our focus on all He has already done. He purchased us with His blood, and has promised us a place in eternity. The Apostle Paul wrote that he was jealous for the Church in Corinth with a godly jealousy, as he had espoused them to one husband, to be presented as a chaste virgin (see II Corinthians 11:2). Apparently, they were straying from the truth, having been beguiled into sin. We are the Bride of Christ. We must be faithful to the bridegroom.

Ancient Hebrew wedding customs are analogous to our Biblical covenant with God. In Jesus' day, there was a bride price system that required a price to be paid for the bride. Divorce was uncommon because of the cost of the wedding. Most people could not afford to get married twice. The first significant parallel we see is that the "bride is chosen," and the marriage contract is sealed with a cup of wine. When we enter into covenant with Jesus Christ, we do so through His blood.

Wine is symbolic of the blood that was shed for our sins. Secondly, the bride can accept or reject the offer. No one is forced to make a covenant agreement with God. However, He has chosen us, and that should be considered to be the best thing that could ever happen to us. God will give our lives purpose that we cannot have without Him.

Fulfilling the will of God in our lives will enable us to cultivate the fruit of peace, in addition to producing viable fruit for His Kingdom. John 15:16 tells us that we have not chosen Him, but He has chosen us so that we may go forth and bear fruit. Therefore, if we are not bearing fruit, we are not fulfilling our covenant agreement with God. Time spent in intimacy with God will produce something in our lives.

Children are a product of intimacy between a husband and wife. It is the will of God for children to be born out of our relationship with Him. The bride and groom were part of an arrangement made by those in authority over them. It is the Spirit of our Heavenly Father that has drawn us so we can become a part of the Bride of Christ. In the Hebrew wedding, the "bride price" was paid by the bride's father. The ultimate price was paid for us when Jesus died on the cross. He became our ransom because He loves us. I Peter 1:18-19 says that we were redeemed with the precious blood of the lamb.

God has purchased the Church with His blood. When we enter into a covenant with Him, we are not our own. When we remain in covenant with Him, we have the assurance that He is with us. We can be sure that His hand is on us for good. We must choose to make our calling and election sure. In Genesis 24:58, Rebekah consents to go with Abraham's servant, even though she has never seen the bridegroom. Although we have not seen Jesus, we were drawn by His Spirit, and accepted His proposal the day we repented and received the Holy Ghost. We love Him because He first loved us. When we love God, and believe He is faithful to His Word, it is not hard to follow the leading of His Spirit. Ephesians 1:13-14, says that we are sealed with the Holy Spirit of promise, which is a pledge towards our inheritance to keep us until the redemption of the purchased possession.

We are that purchased possession. This pledge should be very precious to us. It should be something that we treasure above all else, if we truly love the one who gave it to us. The Spirit of God is a gift for His betrothed. In the Hebrew bride price system, upon committing the groom, "the bride is given gifts". The gifts are a symbol of the groom's love and devotion. The bride is counted worthy by the groom to receive the gifts before the marriage is consummated. In Genesis 24:10, Eliezer brought ten camels laden with gifts to Rebekah. We are sealed with the Holy Ghost (see II Corinthians 1:22). The Holy Ghost comes laden with many different gifts (see I Corinthians 12).

Jesus gives gifts to His bride to enable her to do His will on the earth until He comes for her. As the Hebrew bride uses her wedding gifts to furnish her house, we should use our God-given gifts to fulfill our covenant with the bridegroom. When the bride has these gifts bestowed upon her, along with the groom's name, the bride has everything she needs to prepare for the coming of the groom. The bride is set apart for a period of time while she waits for the return of the groom. We are to live consecrated and Holy lives, while waiting for His return. The Hebrew bride receives a required ceremonial cleansing of water that is called a Mikvah. The Levitical law required cleansing with water. The Bible tells us that immersion in water in the name of Jesus is necessary for the remission of sins (see Acts 2:38). The Hebrew bride is set apart, and wears a veil which symbolizes modesty. Her consecration lets everyone know she is spoken for.

The bride separates herself and comes out from among the single women. We are to live separated lives, and everyone should know our lives are pledged to our bridegroom. We do not live for this world's temporal things. We have hope in a different kingdom. We are called to be Holy because our bridegroom is Holy. The Hebrew bride keeps her oil lamp lit as she waits patiently for the groom to return. It was a custom for the groom to return at midnight. Jesus tells us to be ready because His coming will be like that of a thief in the night.

The groom goes to prepare a place for the bride. In Hebrew wedding customs, the groom's father must give the final okay on the marriage chamber. We read an analogy to this custom in John 14:1-4, which says, I go to prepare a place for you. In my Father's house, there are many mansions... During this time the bride prepares her heart and is consecrated. (See Esther 2:9 for an example of this consecration period). Consecration is an essential part of keeping our covenant relationship with God. We must be holy people, and we must have an understanding of what holiness is.

It has been said that holiness is that ability to walk in a fallen world with love and compassion, being neither affected by or embracing the sin that surrounds one. In fact, someone who is genuinely holy will be able to influence those who are bound by sin. Because holiness is centered in God's love, and love covers a multitude of sins. Holiness is something that comes from within. When our hearts are consecrated to God, holiness will manifest itself outwardly. In the Hebrew wedding, the bride is given a warning before the bridegroom comes for her. A shout is heard, "Behold the bridegroom cometh". After the shout is given, the ram's horn (shofar) is blown. I Thessalonians 4:16-17 says, the Lord himself will descend with a shout, with the voice of the archangel, along with the sound of a trumpet, we will be caught up to meet Him, and be with Him forever.

In that day the ancient prophecy of Jeremiah will be fulfilled that says, again shall the voice of the bride and the bridegroom be heard, and the voice of joy and gladness (see Jeremiah 33:11). These are the promises of God for those that keep His covenant. In the Hebrew wedding, the marriage consummation takes place, and then the honeymoon lasts seven days. Seven is the perfect number of God, signifying completion. During this time everything is revealed, and is naked and open before the groom. II Corinthians 5:10 says that we must all appear at the judgment seat of Christ. This will be our consummation with the Lord. This is the time when we will give account for all that we have done, be it good or bad. The consummation is also a time to become one with the bridegroom. A man leaves his home to become one with his wife (see Ephesians 5:31-32, Genesis 2:24).

In the Hebrew wedding ceremony, when all has been fulfilled, there is a marriage supper. And in Revelation 19:9, there is a marriage supper planned for the Bride of Christ. This will happen one glorious day, and what a wonderful day that will be. It will be worth fighting to overcome tribulation in this life, when we see Him face to face. It is the will of God us to become one with Him, and to be unified in Spirit with the body of Christ.

The Conditions of The Covenant

Jesus prayed for us in John 17:20-23 saying, *"Neither pray I for these alone, but for them also which shall believe on me through their Word; That they all may be one; as thou, Father, art in me, and I in thee, that they also may be one in us: that the world may believe that thou hast sent me..."* (*John 17: 20-21*). Division in the body of Christ has never been the will of God. The enemy uses fear to create walls between those in the body of Christ, and prevent the unity of the Spirit that is necessary for God's power to be manifested.

It should be noted that the word "perfect" used in this scripture by Jesus, literally means to consummate in character. When we become one with the Everlasting Father, the Prince of Peace, and the Mighty God; we are supposed to become perfected, and conformed to His image (see Romans 8:29). The Word "image," used in Romans 8:29, means representation, likeness, and resemblance. When we are in covenant with Jesus Christ, we are supposed to begin to think, act, and resemble Him in character. If we are to be conformed to His character, we must spend time with Him.

Spending time with God demonstrates our faith. This is something we should want to do. Also, if we are to have a relationship with God, we must learn what pleases and displeases Him. We must spend time in the Word of God, worship, and prayer. Without devotional time, we cannot hope to have understanding of the mind of God. Those who faithfully seek after God, have the power of God at work in their lives. God desires to work through humanity to accomplish His will.

However, we limit what He can do through us if our faith is based on religion, and not on a relationship. Religious practices have nothing to do with a covenant relationship as it applies to the New Testament Church. God desires to have a

86

covenant relationship with mankind. Salvation is a work of restoration that is intended to repair the breech caused by original sin. Even though we were dead in sin, if we choose to walk in His ways, the grace of God enables us to sit together with Him in heavenly places (see Ephesians 2:5-6).

God has many great things in store for His Church. However, we must understand that God places conditions on His promises. These conditions will never change. They are recorded throughout Scripture. It is the purpose, plot, and plan of the enemy to blind us, keep us ignorant, and deceived. Not only do we have the enemy to contend with, but the world and our flesh. We can be deceived if we do not hide God's Word in our hearts. It is our responsibility to read God's Word, and know what He requires of us. We cannot expect God to bless us if we violate His commandments. When God spoke to the children of Israel, He told them if you keep my commandments, and walk in my ways, I will bring you to the land I promised to your fathers.

He never said because I am good, gracious, and merciful, I will bring you in. Instead, He told them that He would forgive, but He also would not acquit the guilty (see Exodus 34:6-7). God said to them that if they walked in His laws, they would be blessed, but if they would not, they would be cursed (see Deuteronomy 11:26-28). God is a God of love, but He is also a God of judgment. This is something many do not want to hear, but there are many scriptures to confirm this fact.

There is a spirit in this world that attempts to oppose the work of God. It is complacency, which is born of pride. It works in agreement with fear of commitment, and our flesh. It would have us believe that we can do whatever we want. It says that we live under grace, and not works. If we sin, it will be overlooked because Jesus took care of sin at the cross. Jesus did take care of sin by nailing it to the cross. However, the cross is not without its conditions. To be a disciple (a disciplined one) requires obedience, and a willingness to carry one's cross. The cross is not only for our salvation, but our perfection. Without a desire to be taught, stay under authority, and renew our minds, the cross does not do us any good. The Old Covenant had its law, which was the schoolmaster for Christ (see Galatians 3:24). The New Covenant did not do away with any moral law, but includes even more moral laws that the Holy Ghost will empower us to live by. We must be faithful and obedient. Without a desire to be obedient to the laws of God, grace cannot work in our lives.

The grace of God is contingent on righteousness. In the Holy Scriptures, God made and kept covenants with men who were righteous. They were not perfect, but they had it in their hearts to do what was right. They were men that God could trust to do His will, in spite of their failures. They depended on God, recognized His deity, and had reverence for Him. If we love God, we will want to make things right with Him. Anyone who says they love God, and sins willfully is a liar.

There are some who believe that since we are under grace, sin has no power over us. The truth is, sin that is repented of has no power over us. Grace has been said to be the unmerited favor of God. It is a fact, we don't deserve what God has done for us. We could never repay Him with any act on our part. God simply wants our obedience. We can't expect to have God's favor when we willfully sin. Romans 5:21 tells us that grace reigns through righteousness. Grace can only work when righteousness is present. An example of righteousness is a willingness to repent, continually turning towards God, regardless of our failures. A righteous man gets up seven times. We will never be blameless in this flesh, but we can be righteous in God's eyes through the grace that reigns in a heart that is repentant.

True repentance brings about change. It is more than saying we are sorry. It is continually turning towards God, who will give us the power to overcome our struggles. Repentance is a righteous act. Righteousness is a necessary ingredient in our relationship with God. In the Old Testament, God gave Moses a pattern for the tabernacle plan. God designed everything in the tabernacle plan with shadows of things that would come to pass in the New Testament Church. The mercy seat was symbolic of the grace and glory of God. The mercy seat was placed on the ark of the covenant that held the law of God. Grace and mercy cannot be separated from righteousness.

Righteousness is the throne of grace. Grace will abound as long as we are willing to repent of sin. If we are not, God will not allow us to trample over grace. It is fearful to think that some people live believing that they are protected by the grace of God, while living unrepentant lifestyles, walking where angel's feet wouldn't dare to tread. Angels are sent before God's people, but apparently, they can be offended by sin. Exodus 23:20-22 says, *"Behold, I send an angel before thee, to keep thee in the way, and to bring thee into the place which I have prepared. Beware of him, and obey his voice, provoke him not; for he will not pardon your transgressions: for my name is in him. But if thou shalt indeed obey his voice, and do all that I speak; then I will be an enemy unto thine enemies, and an adversary unto thine adversaries"*. Some angels are spokespersons for God, and others are sent to protect God's people. According to Scripture, there are angels that have different roles. We would be wise not to offend any of these ministering spirits sent by God.

The Conditions of The Covenant

In the book of Jude, we read that satan, and the archangel Michael, contended over the body of Moses. The angel Michael did not bring a railing accusation against satan, but said: "the Lord rebuke thee". The archangel Michael knew that he was speaking on God's behalf. He did not feel the need to argue with or accuse satan. He rebuked him in the name of the Lord. We must have that same boldness. We can possess it when we realize that God will send His angel before us to overthrow our enemies; if we walk uprightly in obedience.

The angel that went before God's people was sent with the power of God's name. The word "name" in Hebrew means a mark of individuality, honor, authority, and character. Angels are sent with the authority and power that has been bestowed on them by God. God told Moses when he was instructed to build the ark of the covenant, to place angels on the mercy seat who would symbolically guard the mercy and righteousness of God. These angels were to by unified, facing one another, with their wings spread. It was revealed in the physical realm, by types and shadows, what was to happen in the spiritual realm. Without righteousness, grace cannot reign (see Exodus 25:19-20).

If we want God's grace manifested in our lives, we must understand the correlation between grace and righteousness. There was a time when the glory of the Lord departed from Israel (see I Samuel 4:21). The glory of the Lord departed because of the sin of Eli, and his sons. The sons of Eli were committing wicked acts regarding the offerings, and fornication in the temple of God. Eli ignored the wickedness of his sons. Their disobedience of God's laws resulted in the ark of the covenant being taken by the Philistines. In the end, the ark was returned because God troubled the Philistines with plagues.

The Conditions of The Covenant

However, Israel was defeated by their enemies because of unrighteousness. Eli's sons were killed in the battle. When Eli heard the news, he fell backwards and broke his neck. In like manner, if we break our covenant with God, we are risking spiritual death. The glory of the Lord, His power, and His favor will eventually depart from our lives. Those who God loves, He rebukes and chastens. If we have the relationship with God that we should have, we can avoid unnecessary tragedy in our lives.

Again, in order to have abundant life, we must not only be obedient, but we must be aware of what our responsibilities towards God are. We cannot fail to take into account the many promises in God's Word that include the word "if". Notice that God said, "But if thou shalt indeed obey his voice, and do all that I speak; then I will be an enemy unto thine enemies, and an adversary unto thine adversaries". God promised physical well being to His people. He promised provision in every area of their lives. He promised to multiply them, to drive out their enemies from before them, and give them possession of the land if they would obey His voice. God's promises, protection, and blessings are dependent on obedience to His Word. The words "but and if" are indicative of this. If we want to have the favor of God in our lives; we must know God's Word, and then act according to His Word. And above all we must pray every day.

God will not ask us to do anything that He will not empower us to do. He will give us the power to tread upon serpents and scorpions, and all authority over the enemy. We must not allow our will and actions to be aligned with the enemy. Our thoughts must be obedient to Christ. The only power the enemy has over us is the power we give him by the choices we make, and what we choose to believe. We cannot expect God to bless willful sin in our lives. If we want forgiveness, we must turn away from sin. God will draw near if we seek Him.

Why wait until crisis hits to seek God? Why not seek His presence every day? Although God is more faithful and merciful than we are, He also is a maker and keeper of covenants. The love and grace of God should motivate us to change for the better. We must allow God to transform us. We can no longer remain servants to sin. Some have misconstrued the scripture that tells us that nothing can separate us from the love of God. God's love is eternal and unconditional, but we are taught throughout the Word of God that sin separates humanity from God. This is fundamental, and the whole reason God stepped down off His throne, manifested Himself in flesh, and died at Calvary. He became sin to defeat it for us.

The Word of God will never change. We must not be deceived. Heaven and earth will pass away, but the Word of God will remain forever. The Word of God tells us that every Word must be established in the mouth of two or three witnesses. Therefore, our doctrine cannot be built upon one verse of scripture about grace. God will judge all iniquity. Scripture teaches that God is not only a God of love, but also a God of judgment in both the Old and New Testaments. We know that God loved David, but he did not let David's sin go unnoticed. However, David received mercy because he was repentant. It was David's contrite heart that touched the heart of God. We have the same ability to move God's heart with humility.

We have been given a remedy for our shortcomings, failures, and fallen nature. Galatians 4:4 says, *"But when the fulness of the time was come, God sent forth his Son, made of a woman, made under the law, To redeem them that were under the law..."*. God Himself became the remedy for us. He has given us the power to become sons of God by adoption through the receiving of His Spirit. There are conditions placed upon becoming a son of God. To be a son means that we care about our Father's business. If we only care about our business, and how circumstances affect us, we won't be likely to wait on God for our redemption. We will live by our laws and conditions, and our mindsets will motivate our actions. If we are driven by our nature and not God's, we will not be able to fulfill His will in our lives, nor will we be able to put on Christ.

When circumstances come our way that are out of our control, it is inherent in our fallen, fearful nature to try and rectify them by our own power. God has a higher purpose at work through trials and tribulations than we can see or comprehend by human reasoning. God does not work in our time frame, and if we do not have patience at work in our lives, we will not wait on God to deliver us out of situations. God asks humanity a question in Isaiah 40:28, saying, aren't you aware that I am the creator of the earth from the beginning to the end? God is speaking to all who will listen, to let them know, that He never grows weary, and His strength never fails. We don't have the power to attain to His level of intellect, wisdom or reasoning. God promises that He will bestow power to those who have none, and strength to those who are weary.

There is hope for those that embrace the promises of God. Even healthy, young men will faint and grow weary, *"But they that wait upon the LORD shall renew their strength; they shall mount up with wings as eagles; they shall run, and not be weary; and they shall walk, and not faint"* (Isaiah 40:31). A condition has been set on the fulfillment of the promise in this verse of scripture. The condition is waiting upon the Lord. The Word "wait" has various applications in the original Hebrew language.

The Conditions of The Covenant

It implies looking for patiently, and binding together as twisting. A rope gets its strength from many different strands that are twisted together. The more strands that are used in this process, the stronger the cord becomes. Different circumstances in our lives can be symbolic of the strands of a rope. When we seek God, and bind ourselves to Him; the circumstances in our lives will increase our strength instead of destroying us. This is because we are walking with the most powerful force in our universe. And love is stronger than death.

We can bind ourselves to God by drawing close to Him during trials and circumstances, instead of seeking pleasures of this world, others, or things. When we seek God during a trial, we are trusting in Him, receiving our strength from Him, and waiting for Him to do the miraculous. Meanwhile, satan attempts to discourage, and waits for our self-destruction.

When we seek God, He will show Himself strong before our enemies. A willingness to wait on God, believing He will strengthen us, will enable us to mount up on eagle's wings. We do not have the power in our humanity to mount up on eagle's wings. Most of us cannot run without becoming weary. The phrase "mount up" has many applications. A few of these are: to arise, restore, and recover. When we wait on God, seeking Him during a trial, we can rise above every situation. When we wait on God, life's tragedies, heartaches, and failures become the things that make us stronger and wiser.

We can recover our strength, and other things we thought were lost. In the end, we will gain something better, and become victorious. This is because the supernatural power that results from the suffering endured, while trusting God, will enable us to fly headlong into any storm that comes our way. Each circumstance we go through pushes us higher, allowing us to make it to the top of every mountain. This is when God's strength is made perfect through our weakness. Waiting on God will enable us to soar like eagles above every storm life brings our way---much to the dismay of our enemies.

We must acknowledge our need for God. We cannot be dependent on our strength. We must recognize that we need His power, regardless of how long it takes for it to be manifested. This requires faith, which means fear must be eradicated. We must believe that no matter what happens to us, God will do right by us. We must believe God can, and will, bring us through any circumstance. Fear will tell us to take matters into our own hands. Waiting on God means we have realized that we are in need of Him. When we walk through valleys, we don't understand, we must look for God in the valley.

While traveling through the wilderness, Moses encouraged the people to trust God. The word "wilderness" means a solitary place. The children of Israel were in a position where they had to rely on God for everything. They were promised that they would be blessed for their faithfulness. However, it was made clear that if they didn't obey, their disobedience would lead to their destruction. Unfortunately, many heard the Word, but did not have faith to make it out of the wilderness. There is danger in not believing the promises of God, and there is danger in walking alone in the wilderness. There were those that did not stay under the authority God had given Moses. God provided the protection of leadership as a covering for the people.

Moses was the meekest of all men (see Numbers 12:3). The enemy and the world were against him from the time he was born, but God had a plan. Moses did not have an easy life, but Moses had a relationship with God. Moses depended on God for everything, and God considered him a friend. While he may have struggled in his obedience, his meekness made him one of the most notable prophets there ever was. Meekness is total dependence on God for everything. With meekness comes the realization that everything has been given to us by God, and ultimately belongs to God.

Our dependence on God allows His strength to be manifested in our lives. Meekness leaves no open door for fear. Those who are meek fear God, not man. Moses, who was raised in a palace, chose to walk in the wilderness with God, leading His people. Moses was a man that waited on God, even though he had human faults. Scripture tells us that Moses was not allowed to enter the land promised to Israel because he disobeyed God's command to speak to the rock. Possibly, it was his frustration with the people that caused him to act in anger, striking the rock, instead of speaking to it (see Numbers 20:12). In spite of his failure, Moses fulfilled the will of God. He maintained his relationship with God.

Although Moses did not enter the land promised to Israel, he appears resurrected elsewhere in scripture (see Mark 9:5). Therefore, we can conclude that he did not lose his place in God's eternal Kingdom. However, a promise made by God was not fulfilled because of his disobedience. Waiting on God means we have faith that God is going to come through for us. Our faith should produce action. We should not be afraid to commit our lives to God, if we believe that saying "God is good", is more than a cliché. Waiting on God means we will be obedient even when obedience doesn't make sense. Waiting for God's answer shows that we are His voluntary servants. It is interesting to note that a synonym of the word "voluntary" is the word chosen.

Mary, the mother of Jesus, was a voluntary servant who was willing to accept the call God placed on her life. She waited on the Lord. Jesus said, many are called, but few are chosen (see Matthew 22:14). Not everyone called will be chosen because not all who are called are willing. Mary, on the other hand, said, *"Behold the handmaid of the Lord"*. The Word "handmaid" means voluntary female slave. We should remember that we entered into God's covenant willfully the day we were baptized. We were chosen, but we must decide to wait on God. Waiting on God is a lifelong commitment that promises the best of outcomes.

The Word "wait," in some of its applications, can be interpreted as "choosing to become a voluntary servant" of the Lord. There is a correlation between the use of the Word "wait" used in Isaiah 40:31, and the Word used in the law of Moses regarding a voluntary servant. The Prophet Isaiah was a man who waited on the Lord. When he saw the Lord high and lifted up, he must have been seeking God with all of his heart. A revelation of the power, majesty, and splendor of God, should give us a desire to become voluntary servants for Him. Again, we must know Him and recognize our need for the power of the Holy Ghost in our lives. Isaiah realized his need for God. He said, *"I am a man of unclean lips"*. When God asked who he could send, Isaiah said, *"Here I am, send me"*.

Isaiah was a voluntary servant. And God did send him, but the road he was sent on was not an easy one. However, the prophet Isaiah had more revelation and insight into the messianic coming of Jesus than any other prophet. We know this by reading his Holy Ghost inspired writings. Even in times of despair, Isaiah waited on the Lord. Isaiah 8:17 says, *"And I will wait upon the LORD, that hideth his face from the house of Jacob, and I will look for him"*. The word "wait" in this verse of scripture, means to adhere to, or through the idea of piercing.

The Conditions of The Covenant

One of the applications of the word "renew" as used Isaiah 40:31, is to pierce or change. Change requires a willingness on our part to pierce through the confusion and deception of destructive thought patterns so that truth can be revealed in every aspect of our lives. We must come to the revelation that our insecurities and fears are not rooted in truth. We must pray in the Holy Ghost so we can be lead by the Spirit of Truth. The Holy Ghost is more powerful than anything satan can bring against us. We must stay connected to God.

When we seek answers from God by connecting with Him in prayer, God's Spirit will sustain us with the powerful force of His love. Also, with peace and truth. When we see things as they really are, or simply make a decision to trust God, renewal will be evident in our lives. When we allow our strength to be renewed God's way, temporary circumstances will not dictate our actions. Instead, the principles of God's eternal Word will motivate us to do things we never thought possible. Could it be that having our strength renewed is dependent upon our willingness to draw near to God?

We can go a little deeper into scripture regarding "voluntary servanthood" in the law of Moses. If a Hebrew servant served six years, he could go free in the seventh. However, if he loved his master, and wanted to stay, Exodus 21:6 says, *"Then his master shall bring him unto the judges; he shall also bring him to the door, or unto the door post, and his master shall bore his ear through with an awl; and he shall serve him forever".* One of the Hebrew meanings of the word "bore" is pierced. When we read this scripture, it may seem barbaric. But it represents a willingness to be bound to one's master forever. Some will shrink back from this idea as they did when Jesus said, *"Verily, verily, I say unto you, Except ye eat the flesh of the*

98

The Conditions of The Covenant

Son of man, and drink his blood, ye have no life in you. Whoso eateth my flesh, and drinketh my blood, hath eternal life...". (John 6:53-54). Many of Jesus' followers walked out on him after this. But there were some who asked, where else will we go? In like manner, Isaiah was not among the fearful.

Although Isaiah was in great difficulty, he chose to wait on God, in spite of the fact that God hid His face because of the spiritual adultery of the people. It is not always easy to trust God when things appear to be falling apart all around us. Especially when we don't understand. Circumstances, the enemy, and our flesh may tell us that giving our life to God has made things worse. The enemy will tell us that we should not commit to things we cannot see or control. The enemy will be there to deceive us when we are down, attempting to make us fear the things we shouldn't, in an effort to keep us from seeking God. There will be times when things have not turned out as we had hoped or prayed they would. However, must choose to remain faithful. We must depend on God's goodness.

This understanding is what Isaiah's hope was based on. Isaiah understood that God is a God of judgment, but he also realized that God is merciful, faithful, and patient towards all who wait on Him. Isaiah 30:18 says, *"And therefore will the LORD wait, that he may be gracious unto you, and therefore will he be exalted, that he may have mercy upon you: for the LORD is a God of judgment: blessed are all they that wait for him".* God has always offered good things to His people. He wants us to have abundant life. A with peace and purpose.

Living for God is the best life. Not only will He return to us so much more than we have forsaken, but He will add to that eternal life. If we will exalt God in our time of trouble, believing He is more powerful than our situation; He will judge life's trials with righteous judgment at the proper time. The judge of all the earth is a fair and just judge. He is more merciful than man, and we can depend on His Word (see I Chronicle 21:13).

We cannot go wrong when we trust Him with our whole heart. He is a refuge and safe place in a time of need. When we wait on God, we become like the servant that didn't want to go his own way, but wanted to remain with his master forever. Trials should not separate us from God, but they should draw us closer. This is what they are designed to do. King David chose to be a voluntary servant of God, and remain in the house of the Lord forever. David was not a man without trials or faults. After he was anointed the king, Saul wanted to kill him.

David was a man of war who fought many battles. David had to overcome the shame and sorrow of sin. He fell into adultery, and committed murder. However, David never stopped seeking God all the days of his life. David did not shrink back from God, nor was he fearful. He obeyed the laws of God, remaining righteous through repentance. In spite of his failures, he was given a light that will never be put out (see I Kings 15:5). Through his lineage came our Lord and Savior, Jesus Christ.

Jesus, who was pierced for our iniquities, chose the cross. He waited on God, was strengthen by God, suffered in this world, and returned to sit on the throne of God. Does this saying cause confusion regarding the revelation of the Mighty God in Christ? No! God intended this to be an object lesson for mankind. The question is, will we do the same? Will we make the choices in life that will take us to that great day when we will rule and reign with Him? Will we hold fast to God? Will we carry our cross? Will we purpose in our hearts to remain faithful, and receive all that God has promised us?

The Conditions of The Covenant

Jesus says, *"Ye are my friends, if ye do whatsoever I command you..."*. The revelation, and promises that we receive from God are a matter of our will. If we are willing to submit our thinking and belief systems to the Word of God, we will never be deceived. We receive revelation from God by choosing obedience in every aspect of our lives. By keeping the conditions of God's covenant, we will not only be joint heirs with Him, but we will also be friends of God, and what could be greater than that.

Chapter Four
The Fearful and the Unbelieving

Revelation 21:8 says, *"But the fearful, and unbelieving, and the abominable, and murderers, and whoremongers, and sorcerers, and idolaters, and all liars, shall have their part in the lake which burneth with fire and brimstone: which is the second death"*. Who are the fearful and unbelieving? And how do we avoid anything the would cause us to be classified as such? These two words, "fearful and unbelieving," imply unfaithfulness and to disbelieve. "Fearful" is defined as being afraid or worried. Unbelieving is described as being skeptical, doubting, suspicious, and questioning. If we doubt God, it is sin. In times of fearfulness or doubt we should pray for a revelation of God's perfect love and His power of forgiveness.

Hebrews 3:12 says, *"Take heed, brethren, lest there be in any of you an evil heart of unbelief, in departing from the living God"*. The word "unbelief" in the original Greek language means, lack of Christian faith, unfaithfulness, and disobedience. Faith should enable us to trust God, and accept some things before we know their outcome. Paul was not speaking to those who didn't know God; Paul was speaking to saints in the Church. He was warning us of the danger of letting doubt and fear enter our minds. He was warning us that a lack of faith could cause us to walk away from God. "Take heed" implies one's perception. He was warning us to be careful of how we perceive all things. He was also warning us against not seeing things as they really are. Wisdom from God will enable us to discern between what is true and false. Unbelief is carnality and rebellion, which opens the door to deception, and opposes truth.

The Fearful and The Unbelieving

In Revelation 21:7, Jesus makes promises to those who overcome. However, He also mentions the fearful and unbelieving. These are not always those who don't know about or have a revelation of God, but those to whom the Gospel has been preached, and won't believe or obey. It is because the Word of God never went farther than knowledge to be written on the tables of their hearts. The fearful and the unbelieving are those who choose to keep their focus on the cares of the world instead of God. Overcomers are believers.

Again, Saul is probably the best example in Scripture of someone who lost out on the promises of God because of his fear and unbelief. Look at the results of embracing fear-based, disobedient thinking. Saul committed the sin that is listed in Revelation 21:8 because of fear. Saul tried numerous times to murder David. Saul wanted to kill David because he was jealous and fearful of him. He knew that David would take the kingdom from him. Jealousy and insecurities are rooted in fear.

Saul was an idolater, especially of his own will. Idolatry is analogous to covetousness, which comes from jealousy. Jealousy is motivated by fear, and can also be a result of unthankfulness. Jealousy is as cruel as the grave (see Song of Solomon 8:6). It will damage, and possibly kill our relationships. Unthankfulness leaves us open to attack from the enemy. We must take on the garment of praise, casting off the spirit of heaviness, if we are to overcome life's battles. And we must not compare ourselves amongst ourselves. We must be sure we are not focusing on others, instead of keeping our focus on God. The fact that Saul never addressed these issues in his life led him deeper into sin, and he became involved in witchcraft. He sought out a woman with a familiar spirit to call up Samuel from the dead. Saul never had the faith to wait on God. Instead, he took matters into his own hands until the end of his life.

Fearfulness will cause us to take matters into our own hands, if we do not choose to believe God is for us, regardless of what is happening. It is easy to have faith when everything is going as we think it should. During times of trial and testing, it may not be easy to wait on God. This is when we are given the opportunity to demonstrate the faith needed to overcome. Remember that he who overcomes will NOT have his name blotted out of God's book of life, but will be clothed in white, and his name will be proclaimed in heaven (see Revelation 3:5).

To "overcome" means to conquer, prevail, and get the victory. God has already given us the victory. But there are things that we must overcome to take ownership of that victory. We live in a society where entitlement is becoming more prevalent every day. We must not embrace this mindset. We must overcome our flesh. We can overcome through a relationship with Jesus, who went before us, and overcame the world. Jesus, the faithful and true witness, has promised a reward to those who overcome.

Keep in mind that these promises are eternal, and our trials are not. Then stop to consider what will happen to those who don't overcome. Considering the cost, and taking into consideration what we stand to lose or gain, should motivate us to rise to the occasion. We must be determined to use the measure of faith God has given us. In order for our faith to grow, we must have a love for God and His ways in our hearts. We must be determined to overcome this world as He did.

When we know Him on a more personal level, His Word will be our bread of life. He will sustain us throughout all eternity with health, peace, joy, and eternal power to reign with Him. Revelation 2:26 says, *"He who overcomes will have power over the nations"*. Revelation 3:12 says, *"He who overcomes will be a permanent fixture in the temple of God"*. Revelation 3:21 says, the overcomer will sit with God on His throne.

With the promise of eternal life, how can we choose to be stubborn? How can we let fear cause us to turn away from God? How can we want to listen to the voice of the enemy, fulfilling his or our will instead of God's? How can we choose the pleasures of sin over the promise of eternal life? Do we love this life so much that we would hold on to worldly things instead of overcoming the enemy through faith? Is our self-will more important to us than God's good and perfect will? Will we choose unbelief over faith, believing God will keep His word? Or will we believe the lies of the enemy?

The enemy discovered long ago that mankind has a problem with flesh, and is susceptible to deception. The enemy can't do anything without a body to work through since he is spirit. The enemy gains access through our carnal mind. Our flesh (self) is the biggest devil any of us will have to overcome. Some people give the devil credit for everything that they do wrong, instead of admitting that the problem lies within them. We are lead astray of our lust, and then we are enticed by the enemy (see James 1:14). We do have an enemy, but we also have choices. Others blame God for all the evil in the world, but never blame mankind's sin or the devil. Often, trying circumstances are a result of bad choices.

The enemy will attempt to get us to blame God for the mess we have made while we were not living right. Our past actions may have left a mess. We may have to reap what we have sown, but God can use our past, and bring us victory. When we overcome our past, and are victorious, it witnesses to a lost world that God is real. This is something that satan does not want.

The Fearful and The Unbelieving

When our actions, or things we say, show the enemy our weaknesses, he will attempt to entice us further into his world of darkness, where fear and deception reign. When life gets us down, we must encourage ourselves in the Lord. Even if we have failed by allowing discouragement to overtake us, we can still turn towards God, and in the end be victorious, if we refuse to let our flesh or the enemy keep us down

The enemy is a master manipulator, who falsifies information; he might offer solutions to problems that are not God's will for us. God's Word has an answer to every problem. Therefore, we must know God's Word. A commitment to getting to know Him is essential to our spiritual health and survival. When we pray, God will answer or more importantly sustain us with His perfect peace. There is protection from the enemy when we stay under the authority of God's Word. If we love God, we will give Him all authority in our lives.

The answer for those who struggle with trusting God, is repentance, submission, and praying in the Holy Ghost. (see Jude 1:20). Fasting will also increase our faith because it puts our flesh down. Our flesh is much more powerful than the devil. Consistent effort is required to keep it under subjection. We must read God's Word, and choose to believe His promises. We should wake every day with the expectation that this is the day we will see God's promises come to pass. The perfect love of God will cast out fear. We must be in a position to receive God's love. Only then, will we be able to love God, and others the way we should. We cannot give what we don't have.

When we love God, and believe in His promises, our actions will prove it. We will not analyze, rationalize, or tempt God because we believe He is faithful, and know He will do right by us. We will do whatever it takes to seek His face. The children of Israel hardened their hearts against God, following their own logic, will, emotions, and desires. Paul said that it was because the Word they heard from God was not mixed with faith. Instead of believing His promises, they refused to trust God. Their actions made it seem they did not believe in His Word or provision. For this reason, they could not enter into the Promised Land. They wandered forty years until those who were disobedient died in the wilderness. No matter how many miracles God performed for them, they did not turn to God for help when the next problem arose. Instead, they complained and wanted to go back to the bondage of Egypt.

God knew what they would do when they faced trouble. In His mercy, He continued to make a way for them. He provided them with leadership, and they had Moses to intercede for them. God knew that fear and unbelief would cause them to turn back. That is why He sent them the long way, through the wilderness, so going back to Egypt would not be easy for them. He did not make everything easy for them. He tested their faith so they would learn to be faithful, be strengthened to endure battle, and learn to trust Him. Trouble has never been meant to drive us back to the world. Trials can and should increase our faith when we overcome them. Trials should cause us to draw closer to God. He is an ever present help in time of need.

We must not allow the enemy or this world to cause us to lose sight of the promises that God has for us. What a tragic thing it is for a child of God to fail to enter into the Promised Land. The children of Israel shut God out because they embraced a lie, believing the words of fearful men instead of the Word God had given them. They did not demonstrate love for God. Instead, they blamed Him for everything, and angered Him with their complaining. Since they didn't trust God to act on their behalf, they minimized His power and authority in their lives. They dethroned God in their hearts and minds, and eventually died in the wilderness. Doubting God's Word has led to many problems for mankind, including a doctrinal error. We never have the authority to change God's Word.

Around 325 AD, a process of events occurred where men began to doubt what God had ordained initially as the plan for His Church. Fearful men started to analyze, doubting the Apostolic doctrine, rewriting the Word of God to according their own reasoning. This is how the faith that was once handed to the saints began to be lost to many. The result has been a loss of power and has caused countless numbers of souls to lose out on the promises of God.

God never intended for His Word to be changed. It is still the will of God for His people to receive the Holy Ghost, be baptized in His name, operate in the gifts of the Spirit, have all their needs supplied, and live an abundant life. However, when God's Word was analyzed and picked apart by men who put it back together according to their reasoning, there was a loss of power. This does not mean God lost His power. It means that God's power is no longer manifested in "some Churches" because of unbelief. Such was the case with the children of Israel.

The children of Israel saw the goodness of the land, and had Joshua and Caleb to encourage them to take possession of what God had promised. However, they chose to listen to an evil report (see Numbers 13:30-33). They decided to put faith in their human reasoning instead of believing what God had promised them. This was in spite of all the miracles, provision, and previous victories God had given them. Psalm 78:32 says, *"For all this they sinned still, and believed not for his wondrous* works". The word "believed" in Psalm 78:32 means to be morally true, to trust, and to go to the right hand.

In scripture, "the right hand" symbolizes strength and power. Jesus says when the son man comes with His angels to divide the nations; the sheep will be placed on His right hand, and the goats on His left (see Mathew 25:33). Sheep are symbolic of the people of God, and goats, of those who don't obey God's commandments. Those on His right hand will be told to enter into the Kingdom of God, and those on his left hand will be told to depart into the everlasting fire that was prepared for the devil, and his angels. Those on the right hand symbolize the righteous and the faithful.

Unrighteousness, which is rooted in unbelief, is what caused the goats to be banished into outer darkness. Matthew 7:21 says, *"Not every one that saith unto me, Lord, Lord, shall enter into the kingdom of heaven; but he that doeth the will of my Father which is in heaven"*. The words of Jesus let us know that we must know God according to His Word. And our knowledge of Him must be mixed with faith. Our faith should lead to a decision to actively seek God and His ways. This remains true even if God's ways seem hard or do not make sense. When things don't make sense, we must seek God for answers, and if none are given, we must stand on His Word by faith.

When we stand on God's Word, we demonstrate our faithfulness, and show the world what we believe. Otherwise, we do not bring glory to God or show this world that we belong to Him. A trial is often an open door for a miracle. Finances are an excellent example of how God proves His Word to us. How many times have we looked at a pile of bills, and then the amount of income we have to pay them, but somehow we are provided with everything we need. God is good even when we are not. We must avoid acting in fear. Financial difficulties handled fearfully might cause us to rob God of the tithe and offering.

If we are afraid to give God a dime on a dollar, we don't believe that God will provide for us. Rationalizing situations according to our knowledge, and ability to understand will hinder our faith. On the other hand, confidence in God's ability to supply our needs will create an atmosphere where God can do the miraculous. When we are struggling financially, physically, or with emotional battles, it may not be easy to believe that God will supply all our needs.

Suffering loss of any kind can cause us to turn away from God in fear and unbelief. We may begin to question why God allowed a particular situation to come into our lives. In times like these, we must continue to believe in the sovereignty, and goodness of God. We need to hold on to what He has done in the past, believing He can do even more. Sometimes God chooses to do a new thing. Faith is believing that no matter what happens to us, God will always do right by us, even though we have not always done right by Him.

Jesus used the parable of the talents to teach the importance of trusting God. The servants who invested their talents were given more, but the fearful and wicked servant, who did not believe he would be rewarded, lost the little he had (see Matthew 25:29). The servant who did not invest his talents was wicked because he didn't believe God would do right by him. His actions accused God of being wicked. Therefore, he counted himself more righteous than God. In the end, the unprofitable servant was cast into the outer darkness where there is weeping and gnashing of teeth (see Mathew 25:30). If that servant had invested the little he had, God would have given him more.

The Fearful and The Unbelieving

We must determine not to be like the wicked servant. We might feel like God has shorted us because we think that God has given others more than He has given us. This can be true of material possessions, positions in the Church, spiritual things, etc. However, if we invest whatever God has given us into the Kingdom, He will provide us with more. He might not always give us what we think we want, but He will give us everything we need. All who came out of Egypt had all their needs supplied, and were destined for the Promised Land.

However, a lack of faith caused many to fall in the wilderness. They did not keep their covenant with God, and never received the promise. This happened to them because they were fearful, and focused on obstacles instead of remembering all the good things God had done for them. It was the will of God to bless Israel, and the generations that would come after them. He made a promise that all families on the earth would be blessed as a result of Abraham's faithfulness (see Genesis 12:3). It was the will of God for the children of Israel to teach His laws to their children so that they would not be rebellious like their fathers. God wanted them to tell of His wondrous works, and transmit faith to the next generation.

Psalm 78:7-10 says, *"That they might set their hope in God, and not forget the works of God, but keep his commandments: And might not be as their fathers, a stubborn and rebellious generation; a generation that set not their heart aright, and whose spirit was not steadfast with God. The children of Ephraim, being armed and carrying bows, turned back in the day of battle. They kept not the covenant of God, and refused to walk in his law"*. It is a shame that Ephraim, being armed and ready to fight, turned back in unbelief. They did not do the will

112

of God. They broke the covenant God had made with their fathers. They never overcame the slave mentality of Egypt.

If God's Church is not diligent, we will make the same mistake as Ephraim. God has equipped His Church with power over the gates of hell. The Bible tells us the gates of hell will not prevail against the Church. God's Church will always be more powerful than the darkness. The question is, will the body of Christ suffer great loss unnecessarily because of stubbornness, rebellion, and unbelief? Will the saints of God listen to the voice of the devil, and believe his lies? Will we allow situations, circumstances, and our flesh to dictate the outcome of the battle? Will we look to this world for answers to our dilemmas or will we seek the mind of God for His will and deliverance? Jesus will have a bride who will be faithful to Him. The question we must ask ourselves is will we allow this world to influence what we believe or will we press on towards the Promised Land?

We must not turn back in the day of battle. We must make use of the power God has given us. If we purpose in our hearts to fight the battles that God sets before us, He will empower us. How powerful would we be if we didn't walk after our own hearts? If we would keep His covenant, and walk in His laws? We must move in the right direction, choosing to believe God, even when everything we see tells us not to. Hoping for something, in spite of how hopeless things look is faith. Having faith requires making a choice to seek after the heart and mind of God, persevering regardless of circumstances.

If we are fully aligned with the mindset of God, we will be able to take vengeance upon disobedience, and overthrow the strongholds that the enemy attempts to establish in our minds. When the Church takes authority over the enemy, the world will take notice of the power of God. The world should not be helping

The Fearful and The Unbelieving

God's people with their problems. God's people should be helping the world, bringing those who are willing, to come out of darkness. We must have the power of God manifested in our lives individually, and as members of the Body of Christ. This is the only way that we are going to make a difference in this world. God's Church must stand as that city upon a hill. We must be a shining beacon in a dark world.

Faith will enable us to stand when nothing seems to be happening, and we seem to be getting nowhere. Faith will enable us to wait on God's timing. Time constraints don't hinder God. He is the Holy One that inhabits eternity. When we seek God for help with our problems, and He doesn't answer the way we want Him to, we sometimes turn away from God in search of alternative solutions. We are in need of patience, meaning endurance or the ability to wait, so that after we have obeyed God, we might obtain the promise (see Hebrews 10:36).

The word "promise" literally means to pledge, and a divine assurance of good. We must remember that His ways are higher than our ways, He always keeps His Word, and our concept of time is much different than His. His timing is always right. And He knows what is best for us. He knows what the future holds. We must choose to have faith in God whether He gives us our way or not. Those who choose to wait on God find that His plans are best. Our ways are not best because they are a result of following our deceitful hearts.

Those who rebel, choosing not to put their trust in God, end up doing things their own way without the help of God. God will not stop us from following our own path, but He will not go with us. A road traveled without God is a road we do not want to take. We start down a treacherous highway when we follow thoughts of doubt and uncertainty. These will cause us to draw back from

114

The Fearful and The Unbelieving

God. Hebrews 10:38-39 says, *"Now the just shall live by faith: but if any man draws back, my soul shall have no pleasure in him. But we are not of them who draw back unto perdition; but of them, that believe to the saving of the soul"*. Jesus says that any putting their hand to the plow, looking back, are not worthy of the Kingdom of God. We must count the cost, consider the reward, and never look back. We cannot be bound to the past.

We must stand fast in the liberty we have been given from sin. The enemy deceives many into believing that God's laws are bondage. But we must not live by that belief system. We must press forward in our faith to receive the hope of glory, and salvation of our souls. To "drawback" means cower or shrink, shun, and be timid. When the apostles faced persecution, they prayed, and were filled again with the Holy Ghost (see Acts 4:31). When they were filled with the Holy Ghost, they went out and spoke the Word of God boldly. If we are full of the Holy Ghost, praying every day, we will be bold in our faith. We will not succumb to fear because we have something greater within us than circumstances or the temporal things of this world.

Nehemiah was a man who understood that the enemy would use fear to keep him from doing the will of God. In Nehemiah's day, Jerusalem was in heaps of rubble and ruin. Nehemiah prayed and fasted over the state of the Holy city. The walls were burned down, and the city destroyed because of the people's disobedience. Nehemiah was the king's cupbearer. While he was performing his duties, king Artaxerxes noticed Nehemiah's sad countenance, and asked him what troubled him. Initially, he was afraid to answer, but then told the king he was distraught because of the destruction of the city. The king asked him to make a request, and the Bible says he prayed to the God of heaven (see Nehemiah 2:4), and made his request. The king granted him permission to repair the city. As soon as the restoration process began, there was resistance from the enemy. It is interesting to note some definitions of the word "restoration": The action of returning something to a former, owner, place, or condition; the return of a hereditary monarch to a throne, head of state, or a regime to power (Merriam Webster). We are to be kings and priests to our God.

It is not unusual for the enemy to attempt to stop any restoration process. While God is putting back together the broken pieces of our lives, the enemy will come to discourage the rebuilding process with fear, doubt, and confusion. The enemy will attempt to hinder us from fulfilling the will of God. The Bible says that Sanballat and Tobiah were very upset when they learned that Nehemiah had begun a restoration process for the children of Israel. God, in His mercy, made a way to restore what sin had destroyed. God is in the restoration business. When choose to let God restore our lives, the enemy will attempt to stop the restoration process with fear and intimidation.

The enemy did not hinder Nehemiah. He encouraged the people to have the faith needed to work at the restoration process. As the people strengthened their hands to do the work, Sanballat, Tobiah, and Geshem came to torment and discourage them. The Bible says that they made fun, and cast doubt upon them, in order to discourage them from doing the work. However, the people chose not to listen to the voice of the enemy, and began rebuilding the walls of the city. When their enemies learned the city was being restored, they discouraged them by saying what they built was not strong enough, and would not endure (see Nehemiah 4:3). The devil will try to intimidate us into thinking we can't make it, or that we are wasting our time; he will try to cast doubt on the restoration process in our life.

The Fearful and The Unbelieving

The enemies of God's people initially used subtle tactics to discourage further restoration of the city, and when those didn't work, they resorted to mockery and open confrontation. However, the restoration continued because the people had a mind to work. While the breaches were being closed, the enemies of God's people fought against them, but God's people continued to work together. They were unified in their effort to close up the breeches of the wall that gave access to their enemies.

The enemy does not want the breaches closed up in our lives because that is the only way he can gain access to our souls. An analogy can be made between the enemies' strategies now, and strategies used by the enemy in Nehemiah's day. The enemy hasn't changed. Therefore, we can anticipate his attacks when we know the Word of God, and apply it to our lives. We must gird up the loins of our minds with truth, putting on the full armor of God. We must sure up any breaches in our armor.

The walls that were built around a city were meant to keep enemies out. The enemy wants to create breaches in our minds with doubt and intimidation. Not only to keep God's will from being accomplished through the restoration of our lives, but to send us down the path to hell by enticing us with many distractions. He looks for our weaknesses to determine how he can influence us into breaking our covenant with God.

Circumstances in life have a way of robing us our strength. Then the enemy will attempt to move in for the kill. If satan can influence us with fear while we are down, he can create illusions in our minds that affect our thought processes and reasoning. If we are confused, it is easy for doubt to enter our minds. We must not let satan intimidate us with the past or present bad circumstances. If we are intimidated because of past failures, or fear of the unknown, we will not have the boldness or stamina to do what God has called us to do. This was the intent of those that withstood Nehemiah.

Nehemiah's enemies became very angry when their intimidation tactics did not work. They came to fight against Jerusalem to hinder the work. At this point, Nehemiah, and the Jews that were with him prayed to God. They also set a watch day and night (see Nehemiah 4:9). They did not stop to eat or do other things. They came together as a united force. While some rested, others stood in their stead against the enemy. This is what we must do if we are to overcome the enemy. We must be prayerful, we must believe the Word of God, and always be on guard against the deception of the enemy.

We can't allow him to hinder our progress. We should not fear the enemy, but we cannot be ignorant of his devices. If he perceives that we are a threat to his kingdom, he will work against us. If we are ignorant of satan's devices, he will have an advantage over us. Nehemiah realized that his enemies were attempting to use fear to cause him to fail God, and to bring him under their control. They wanted Nehemiah, and the children of Israel to remain a reproach to the other nations. They did not want the God of Israel to be glorified.

They knew if they could keep God's people under the control of shame and fear, they would never do His will or glorify Him. They wanted to destroy the people of God by causing them to sin. Nehemiah 6:13 says, *"Therefore was he hired, that I should be afraid, and do so, and sin, and that they might have matter for an evil report, that they might reproach me"*. Nehemiah was not ignorant of the methods his enemies were using against him. He prayed, asking for God's intervention against those who attempted to hinder the work. Nehemiah did not allow the restorative work to be hindered.

118

The Fearful and The Unbelieving

When the restoration was complete, those who opposed God's people were not heard from anymore. The people knew that it was the work of God. The enemy never wants restoration in our lives because this brings glory to God. If we refuse to allow circumstances to stop us, it will shut the mouth of the enemy. God deserves all the glory in the good times and the bad. This is where the power God gives us must be utilized to pull down strongholds that the enemy is always attempting to erect in our minds. We must not allow ourselves to be intimidated by lies that come from the kingdom of darkness.

Fear is a catalyst for sin. Fear caused Jeroboam to sin, and lead many astray (see I Kings 12:26-30). Fear should not motivate the leaders of God's people. Jeroboam, one of Israel's wicked kings, prevented the people from going to offer sacrifices in Jerusalem because he was afraid that the kingdom would return to the house of David. Jeroboam feared the king of Judah. Instead of allowing the people to go to the house of God, Jeroboam made two calves of gold and presented them to the people; telling them that it was too hard for them to go to Jerusalem. Jeroboam said to the people, worship these calves; they are your gods that brought you out of Egypt.

The Bible tells us that this sin affected all the people. Unrepentance will eventually cause death, and will result in shame in our emotions. When shame and fear are present, our thought processes are negatively affected, which can result in sin. Sin opens the door for shame and fear, which results in more sin, and the hopelessness of sin opens the door for depression. We have the ability to draw near to the One who has removed shame for us, along with the sting and fear of death. Jesus, our Lord and Savior. Of His Kingdom, there shall be no end.

Chapter Five
The Fear of the Lord

The Bible tells us that the fear of the Lord is the beginning of wisdom. Surely we should reverence God because of who He is, but our greatest motivator should be love. We have a lot of reasons to love God. First of all, He loved us when we were still sinners. God loves us unconditionally. He wants to give us abundant life. He wants us to be a part of His Kingdom in spite of our shortcomings, faults, and failures. He became sin and shame for us, nailing these things to the cross. He has spoiled every principality that triumphed over us. He has made an open show of these things, and has blotted out the handwriting that was written against us.

In Biblical times, when an army defeated an enemy, they would march the defeated army, stripped of their weapons, through the streets of the city for all to see. This was so the people would know they no longer had to fear this enemy. This is what the term, "making an open show" meant in the physical realm. Today it applies to us in the spiritual realm. Jesus has defeated every principality and power. He has given us victory over them all. The enemy has no power over our lives, unless is is given to him. The enemy of our soul has no power against us, other than the hope we will be intimidated, believe his lies, focus on our past, and live in a state of fear.

We may all face things that make us question where God is, or what His purpose is in our lives. We must choose to believe we are fearfully, and wonderfully made. The word "wonderfully" used in Psalm 139:14 means set apart or separated. God has a purpose for all of our lives. Nobody was created by accident. No matter what we are going through, He has already gone before us and has overcome. Faith should come from our hearts, and be demonstrated by our actions. If we truly love God, and believe in Him, we won't analyze His Word. Our love for God should carry us through any struggle we may have with our faith because love is the strongest force that exists. Love is stronger than the deception of our enemy, and will be the catalyst that lifts us out of life's valleys, giving us strength to climb to the mountain top. We are able to overcome because we believe that He loves us. Our faith will keep us grounded in His Word, and we can wear the full armor of God with confidence. God's love is stronger than death or fear. Eternal life is available to us all because of love.

Scripture reveals to us that humanity's first experience with fear was the fear of death. It is possible that fear can get dominion in our minds because of an underlying fear of death or loss. God said, *"But of the tree of the knowledge of good and evil, thou shalt not eat of it: for in the day that thou eatest thereof thou shalt surely die"* (Genesis 2:17). Therefore, on the day that Adam and Eve ate from the tree that was forbidden to them, not only was their innocence gone; they also became aware that they would die. Until the time that the devil approached Eve, it appears that man did not live with doubt, shame, or fear of any kind. Because of original sin, we must fight to overcome these things. Most importantly we must learn to discern between what is true and false. Wisdom can be defined as the ability to know the difference between what is true and false. If we are in need of wisdom, the Bible tells us that we must not be afraid to ask God. We must turn towards Him, not away from Him. Every step away from God is a step into deception.

When we dwell on things that make us afraid, worrying about something that might happen, our thoughts can become blown out of proportion. This is when we can be deceived into believing things that aren't true. It is possible to relive a traumatic experience over and over again in our minds. This is Post Traumatic Stress Disorder (PTSD) defined. When a traumatic experience has happened, it can be hard to move on from it mentally. It can be easy to believe it will happen again. While repeated actions can produce the same negative results, we cannot allow fear to torment us with the past. We must choose not to live in the past mentally. We must be diligent in refusing the false illusions that fear will attempt to form in our minds, refusing to let our future be shaped by past trauma.

While is good to learn from our past, we cannot let it cripple us. We must refuse to dwell on thoughts that bring past trauma into the present. These thoughts rob us of the peace God wants us to have. God does not want us to be fearful of things that have already happened. God has already defeated our enemies. Why should we live in fear? In this life, we will have tribulation, but we are promised victory.

As long as we are living according to the principles God has set for us, we do not need to be afraid of a defeated enemy. Scripture teaches us of the deceptiveness of fear. Psalm 53:5, which says, *"There were they in great fear, where no fear was: for God hath scattered the bones of him that encampeth against thee: thou hast put them to shame because God hath despised them"*. Although God's people had enemies that surrounded them, God had already defeated their enemies. They believed in an illusion instead of the power of God, even though they had been a witness to many great miracles. It is tragic when the people of God do not believe His Word. We might think of unbelievers as those who deny God's existence. However, scripture defines the unbelieving as those who do not trust in the promises and goodness of God. God is hindered from working good in the lives of believers who don't trust Him.

King David stated that God looked down from heaven at the children of men to see if any had understanding of God or did seek Him. Jesus asked a similar question when he taught the parable of the unjust judge (see Luke 18). He posed this question, *"if an unjust man would do right by a woman, who was diligent in her request; won't God, who is righteous, do right by His people"*. Then He asked, upon my return, will I find faith upon the earth? Will He find us faithful, or will He find us worried about what has happened, might happen, or will happen? Will He find us playing Church or will He find us using the gifts He has given us to further His Gospel and Kingdom?

King David, under the inspiration of the Holy Ghost, lamented, *"all have backslidden, and have done wickedly. There is none that have called upon God. These are men with no knowledge or wisdom. They do not consider God or His mighty outstretched arm. They have no fear of the Lord. Therefore, they are deceived and have become fools. They go about and do what they want, according to the desires of their wicked hearts"*. David prayed, *"Oh that the salvation of Israel were come out of Zion! When God bringeth back the captivity of his people, Jacob shall rejoice, and Israel shall be glad"* (Psalm 53:6). David prayed that deliverance would come to those who were deceived. They had put their faith in the enemy instead of God. They believed in their own imaginations instead of the power of God. What a tragedy it is to know of His great salvation and delivering power, yet live as a prisoner to fear and deception.

The Fear of the Lord

There is no reason that any child of God should live in fear of any kind. If we believe in God, and walk in the fear of the Lord, angels will be encamped around us (see Psalm 34:7). What was accomplished at Calvary provided all the deliverance we need from the fear of death. Hebrews 2:14-15 says, *"Forasmuch then as the children are partakers of flesh and blood, he also himself likewise took part of the same; that through death he might destroy him that had the power of death, that is, the devil; And deliver them who through fear of death were all their lifetime subject to bondage".* God literally manifested Himself in the flesh in order to become like us so that He could shed His blood for the remission of our sins. He conquered death for us so that we could have eternal life. Therefore, He removed the power death had over us. We must not let His sacrifice go in vain.

Violation of God's commandments has brought devastation to the human race. God's ways are perfect. There is a highway of holiness available to us. There will not be any ravenous beasts, or fools, only the redeemed of the Lord will travel this highway. There will be no sorrow, fear, or sin. If we have a love for wicked ways, how can we desire a righteous Kingdom where there is no wickedness? If we have run with the footmen, and can't keep up with them, how will we make it in the swelling of the Jordan? (see Jeremiah 12:5)

If we can't live by God's laws in the Church Age; can we make it if things really get rough? What if we had to make a stand for what is right against fierce opposition? Are we able to take a stand for what is right against our families? If we believe what the Bible says, we know one day the Church will be raptured. If we aren't strong enough to fight now, will we be strong enough to survive the tribulation period (see Revelation

7:14). It is better to live righteously, not caught up in the cares of this world, and fight for our relationship with God.

We must be faithful to our covenant with God. And we must have balance in our thought life. We do have to be concerned with some aspects of this life, but must not put the cares of this life in the forefront of our minds, totally focused on worldly things instead of the things of God. We must also take our eyes off people. Some are so dependent on people that, should they be disappointed by others, they will leave the Church. We should not be more dependent on people than we are on God.

God should be the reason we attend Church. Above all, we should not trust in our own devices more than we trust in God. Surely Eve thought she was making the right choice, by following her own heart, when she helped bring about the fall of man. When she followed her desire for the temporal things of the world, the fallen angel was able to trick her, and open up her mind to worldly thinking. The enemy's intent was to make Eve believe that she did not need God. Thus humanism was birthed. Our enemy will always need a body to work through.

According to Frederick Edwords, of the American Humanist Association, "Humanism whether religious or secular, "is usually without a god, without a belief in the supernatural, without a belief in an afterlife, and without a belief in a "higher" source of moral values. Some adherents would even go so far as to suggest that it is a religion without "belief" of any kind··· knowledge based on evidence being considered preferable. Furthermore, the common notion of "religious knowledge" as knowledge gathered through non-scientific means, is not generally accepted in Religious Humanist epistemology" (Edwords 1989). In short, humanism believes that mankind is the highest form of being. While this doctrine attempts to elevate mankind to a status equal to or above God, at the same time it reduces mankind down to the level of animals with no soul. As wrong as this may seem, if we choose sin over our covenant with God, placing no value on our souls; are we any better?

Humanism, a fear based doctrine, would have us void of faith in anything other than self. Humanism teaches that we are our own gods. It is without hope or redemption of any kind. In essence, it is the belief that there is no understanding, judgment or wisdom higher than man's intellectual ability. This is a very dark way of thinking that God never wanted mankind to have. And who was it that wanted to ascend higher than God?

Humanism was interjected into Eve's thought pattern when she was tempted with worldly wisdom through what has been called the three points of sin. I John 2:15 says, *"For all that is in the world, the lust of the flesh, and the lust of the eyes, and the pride of life, is not of the Father, but is of the world"*. Desire caused her to listen, and then look for something she didn't have. Then doubt caused Eve to put her trust in the voice of the enemy.

She was no longer concerned with what God had said. And Adam, who had been told not to eat from that particular tree before God created Eve, was given dominion in the garden, and did nothing to prevent her deception. She believed the enemy's lie, and lusted after worldly wisdom. She looked, listened, and acted upon her fleshly desire. Scripture informs us that Adam was there with her. Therefore, since he didn't prevent her, it would seem that he had the same desire (see Genesis 3:6).

Why didn't God want His most treasured creation to access the tree of the knowledge of good and evil? God allowed them access to everything else, but He prohibited this one thing.

The Fear of the Lord

Perhaps it was because God wanted to test their faithfulness by giving them a choice to obey or disobey. Could it be since love is a choice, that God hoped His most treasured creation would choose to love and obey Him? Why this one restriction? Could it be that God would have preferred that mankind be ignorant concerning evil? It is written, *"I would have you wise unto that which is good, and simple concerning evil"* (Romans 16:19). While we are encouraged to seek God for wisdom, "the principal thing", we are told not to seek worldly wisdom or follow after the beggarly elements of this world. He wants us to have knowledge of higher things, eternal things, the things that are of His Kingdom. He wants us to take dominion over sin.

God knows the wicked ways of satan, and the destruction and despair that existed before He spoke restoration into a void situation. God knew that if Adam and Eve lost their innocence by obtaining the knowledge of good and evil, it would give the enemy access to their minds. The enemy has been able to influence mankind's thinking ever since the first covenant between God and mankind was broken.

When we step out of covenant with God, a door is opened in our mind for the enemy to bring error, confusion, and wicked thoughts. We must remember the condition of the world before God spoke into it. Imagine a world entirely void of the presence of God. If we step out of covenant with God by making willful decisions, we cause the Spirit of God to withdraw from us. Without God's Spirit, we are left with the limited ability afforded to us by the wisdom of this world. The wisdom of this world does not include God or His Word. It is an understanding void of the knowledge of God, and is based on the fundamentals, teaching, and mindsets of this world.

128

The Fear of the Lord

Paul warned us not to be deceived. Colossians 2:8 says, *"Beware lest any man spoil you through philosophy and vain deceit, after the tradition of men, after the rudiments of the world, and not after Christ"*. The word "rudiment" implies a system, order, and a way that things are done. The word "spoil" means to lead away as booty or seduce. "Booty" is something captured during a war by an enemy. We must be determined not to become a prey of the enemy. There is a seducing spirit in this world that wants us to dismiss the laws of God so that we will go along with the world's system. The systems of this world are at work to bring us out of covenant with God.

God's Word is the anchor that will keep us from being swept away by deception. We have the admonishment that there will be those who will try to teach their way of thinking, attempting to pass it off as God's. The sacred Word of God has been preserved for all time for the salvation of men's souls. Belief, which leads to obedience, brings us into an everlasting covenant with Him. The world's systems are rooted in unbelief, and if followed, will lead us away from God into captivity. The Bible warns us that earthly wisdom is not from above. This truth is evident in the actions of those who follow this world's ways. God's Word admonishes us that if we are wise, we will not embrace the wisdom or philosophies of this world. James 3:13 says, *"Who is a wise man and endued with knowledge among you? let him shew out of a good conversation his works with meekness of wisdom"*.

Worldly wisdom, or for all practical purposes, we can call it worldly thinking (humanism), leads mankind away from faith to be influenced by fear, which results in many destructive behaviors. There is no true peace in following the world's ways.

The Fear of the Lord

In the end, when we are totally responsible for who we are, according to this world, strife comes. In the world's system, we have to compare ourselves amongst ourselves, struggling to find purpose and self-worth. If we are dependent on our own abilities, instead of allowing ourselves to become who God created us to be, any failure can lead to destruction.

God, who is the Alpha and the Omega, and knows all things, foresaw the outcome of man's quest for knowledge beyond what God had given him. Parents can relate to this. They normally don't want their children influenced by wrong teaching because they know it will lead to their destruction. God feels the same way about His children. It is in our nature to want to analyze everything, to be willful, and do things our own way. Although this may be our desire, it is not what is best for us. The end thereof is death and destruction. James exhorted us that if we are wise, we must demonstrate our wisdom through our actions. The Word "conversation" as is used in scripture, means behavior. Our behavior must be in line with the Word of God.

Worldly wisdom has no place in God's Church. James wrote to the early Church to let them know that if they possessed knowledge and wisdom of God, their behavior should demonstrate humility and obedience to the Word of God. If there was bitterness and jealousy among them, he told them it was apparent that the wisdom they received was not of God, but of the world. He admonished them not to reject the truth by embracing the ways of the world, which are not of God. He also told them not to give false witness against the truth through their actions. In other words, he told them not to be hypocrites.

We present false evidence against God's Word when we don't live what we claim to be. God's Word does not allow for strife, contention, confusion, or jealousy. These things come from the human mind, and our fallen nature, which can be influenced by satan's kingdom. We must take authority over worldly wisdom with obedience to the Word of God. If we don't, we bear false witness against the truth. There is no room for pride or shame, which are rooted in fear.

Knowledge of, and obedience to, the Word of God will result in a teachable spirit, good works, peace, and righteousness. It will put a stop to confusion and bring order. It will also put a stop to hypocrisy. Christian hypocrisy is a serious problem in the Church today. When those outside the Church see inconsistency, disobedience, and fearfulness in "Churched" people, it casts doubt on God's Word.

The word "hypocrisy" means to have double standards and to be insincere or two-faced. James also used the Word "partiality". This word means to, doubt, stagger and waver. None of these actions or thoughts are from the Word or Mind of God. God never wavers, He is not a respecter of persons, and He never doubts. He will judge, but even God doesn't judge a man until he dies. We don't have the right to judge any man. But we often do, when we are no better ourselves. All unforgiveness is rooted in pride, and is judgment. The enemy desires to destroy unity in any way he can and bring division.

These evil mindsets creep into our lives when we permit ideas that do not come from God's Word to influence us. If we embrace earthly philosophy, we are no longer under God's authority; we are under the authority of this world. The Bible tells us that satan is the prince of this world. Our behavior is a testimony of whose influence we are under. We are supposed to be a light in a dark world, a city set upon a hill. How can we be light when there is no distinct difference between those who claim to be Christian and those who do what is right in their own eyes. Many lack respect for Christianity because of the double standards they see Christians living.

There are many causes for Christian inconsistency. One of the biggest is fear of rejection. Many would rather blend in with the crowd than stand up for what is right. The problem is that when we are lukewarm, trying to walk both sides of the fence, we don't receive approval from God, and we don't earn the respect of our fellow man either. Even if non-believers don't agree with Christianity, they have more respect for someone who is willing to stand for what they believe, than for a double minded individual. This is a saying that rings true, "if you don't' stand for something, you will fall for anything".

When people do not want to take a stand for what is right, they end up living a double standard. They end up giving into situations that cause them to fall, and portraying an image that tells the world that the power of God isn't real. This is not the testimony that we want to present to the world. This is why many unbelievers think that Christians are weak, and use Christianity as a crutch to lean on.

Scripture and history tell us that the Church was born on the day of Pentecost in 33 AD (see Acts, chapter 2). God wants His Church to be a Church who will stand against the gates of hell. How can those in the Church prevail against the enemy if they are in unity with him? A kingdom that is divided cannot stand. If there is division, double-mindedness, and strife among us, how can we take a stand against the enemy? When we allow our fears, insecurities, and things from the past to dominate our present and future; we cannot conquer the enemy because we have not put disobedience out of our lives. This must be accomplished before we can take revenge on disobedience.

This vengeance against disobedience begins when our thoughts are brought under the authority of God's Word. We can't allow the enemy to dictate what we believe. When we start to believe in the false evidence that satan has presented, we are no longer under God's authority. It is at this point that fear becomes a stronghold that will reveal its ugly face in our lives. This is what happens when we choose not to believe in the Word of God. Obedience is an indication of faith, while disobedience is evidence of unbelief. Those that believe will act accordingly.

We must be not only hearers of the Word but also doers of the Word. To be a doer of the Word, we need a spirit of humility. A spirit of humility will enable us to be in submission to the Spirit of God. God cannot reveal His mind to individuals who exalt their thinking above His. This is rebellion, witchcraft, and what got satan kicked out of heaven. God did not allow it then, and He will not allow it now. It is a fact that our thinking will always affect our behavior.

If we are to be children of light, we must be able to discern between wisdom that comes from God, and the influences of wisdom that comes from earthly sources. We cannot be indoctrinated with the knowledge that does not include the fundamental teachings from the Word of God. This is not to say we should not be educated. But we must not leave out the moral teachings from the laws of God. If we God out, it is evident that we are being influenced by worldly wisdom. We must not be ignorant of the influence of the world or the enemy.

The word "wisdom," used in the New Testament, implies knowledge or judgment that is either worldly or spiritual.

The Fear of the Lord

Webster's Concise Dictionary defines "wisdom," or being wise, as the ability to judge soundly concerning what is true and false. When our thinking is being influenced by the mindset of this world, we will be deceived. God didn't want mankind to have the knowledge of what was evil because He knew it would lead to the breach of the covenant He made with Adam, and mankind's exile from the garden. God, in His sovereignty, foresaw the rebellion against His first commandment that would enslave humanity when they received the knowledge of evil. With the knowledge of wrongdoing comes the realization that we have been trespassed against.

It is then that it becomes easy to rise up in judgment against others and God. When we judge our brother, we also judge God who created him, and are in opposition to truth. It is written, *"if ye have bitter envying and strife in your hearts, glory not, and lie not against the truth"*. God's Word is truth. Bitterness, jealousy, and divisions come from a heart that is lifted up in pride, and is far from God.

This rebellious mindset is why satan was thrown out of heaven, and is a cause of confusion and disunity in families, and in the Body of Christ. These things have fear as a root. Bitterness is rooted in fear. When we dwell on what someone did, worrying that they will get away with it, we become their judge. When we judge, we are questioning God's ability to handle the matter, and we are forgetting that we are also trespassers.

Another pitfall caused by fear is jealousy. A contributing factor to jealousy is worrying about what we don't have, and unthankfulness. Jealousy will always result in division. Jealous people are dangerous people. Also, fear of others, who are different, can cause division when we don't understand people of different nations and cultures. God knew that His Word was the only knowledge Adam and Eve needed, and His Word is the only truth we need. On judgment day, the philosophies of this world won't mean a thing.

Knowledge from the enemy will lead to every wicked and evil work. It will also lead us away from God and salvation. Pilate asked Jesus a question, *"What is truth?"* Pilate didn't realize truth was standing right before him. He was influenced by Roman law, and the minds of the people. Although he did help carry out the plan of God, he was ignorant of the fact that he was in the presence of the Mighty God, the Everlasting Father, and the Prince of Peace. We must be careful that we don't allow humanism or carnal mindsets to separate us from God.

The greatest commandment ever given says, *"Hear, O Israel; The Lord, our God, is one Lord: And thou shalt love the Lord thy God with all thy heart, and with all thy soul, and with all thy mind, and with all thy strength: this is the first commandment. And the second is like, namely this, Thou shalt love thy neighbour as thyself. There is none other commandment greater than these" (Mark 12:29-31).* This is what is most important to God. The mindset of the world, which results in envying and strife, keeps us from fulfilling God's Covenant.

We cannot keep our Covenant with God when we have hatred or jealousy towards our brother in our heart. The Bible tells us that jealousy is cruel as the grave and akin to death (see Song of Solomon 8:6). The Word of God tells us that whoever hates his brother is as a murderer (see I John 3:13). We don't have to go far in this day and age to see hatred at work in our society. Most look out for number one. II Tim 3:2 says, *"For men shall be lovers of their own selves".* This is one of the biggest problems many have today. The central theme of humanism is self, which separates mankind from God. God is love, and His love is unconditional, but He is also a respecter of human will.

Even if we fulfill every other aspect of God's law, but have hatred, jealousy, and bitterness in our heart, we fall short of fulfilling God's law. James 2:8-10 says, *"If ye fulfill the royal law according to the scripture, Thou shalt love thy neighbour as thyself, ye do well: But if ye have respect to persons, ye commit sin, and are convinced of the law as transgressors. For whosoever shall keep the whole law, and yet offend in one point, he is guilty of all".*

Bitterness, rebellion, and shame did not exist in the heart of man until man sinned. When man chose to willfully disobey God's law these destructive forces entered the heart of man. Because God so loved the world, He came to defeat these evil forces, which are destined for the pits of hell. It is our choice to have a conscience void of offense or have a root of bitterness in our hearts. Jesus foretold of a day when men's hearts would be cold, they would hate one another, and false prophets would deceive many. With the people of God, it must not be so.

While it is clearly stated in scripture that we must love and forgive others, the commandment to love one's self is often overlooked. Rejection of one's self is shame. Shame and fear work hand in hand to prevent a child of God from doing the will of God. Our insecurities about ourselves come from our emotions. Shame is a human emotion, while fear, as stated earlier, is a spirit that is not from God. The enemy is skillful at working on our human emotions and fallen nature with fear and intimidation; attempting to infiltrate our thought life with poison, reminding us of our failures, words we said, or that someone else said, and events of the past. He wants to keep us in fear when there is no reason to fear.

It is the goal of our enemy to keep us from fearing God, and get us to fear temporal things that are no eternal threat to us. This is an attempt to destroy our faith so we will sin. If we allow him access to our minds, he will attempt to control us through our thought life, and put a yoke on us that will prevent us from doing the will of God. Not only that, if we allow him in, he will begin to control our actions.

The only way he can accomplish this is if we choose to believe things that aren't true. Things that go against the Word of God, including things sound good to our flesh. The truth must be valued above all else. It must be more important than riches, houses, or lands. It is something that must be desired above rubies or gold. It is something that must bought and never sold.

Chapter Six
Buy the Truth and Sell It Not

Church History tells us that around 90 AD, the Church experienced severe persecution. While Apostolic teaching was not totally lost, doubt arose as to the accuracy of what was originally penned, and taught by the apostles. This lead to much debate among Greek philosophers regarding the validity of Monotheism. In an effort to defend Christianity from the debaters, and also to please the people; they formed what they asserted to be a "divine philosophy". Thus, philosophy became intermingled with divine inspiration. "With the Greek Apologists, the literature of the Church addresses itself for the first time to the outside world and enters the domain of culture and science" [Quasten, Patrology Vol. I, p.186]. The Apostle Paul, inspired by the Holy Ghost, warned the Church in Colossians 2:8-9, *"Beware lest any man spoil you through philosophy and vain deceit, after the tradition of men, after the rudiments of the world, and not after Christ. For in him dwelleth all the fullness of the Godhead bodily"*. Unfortunately, these philosophers did not receive revelation from Paul's writings.

These men, who were believed to be more educated than the Apostles, began to analyze and question the original writings, which lead to a dissolution of apostolic teaching among some, the inclusion of pagan teachings, and the introduction of a triune god. This occurred after the death of the last apostolic fathers. It was believed that because the Greek Apologists were educated men, and the apostles were supposedly uneducated, they could better interpret the scriptures. The result was a loss of truth. And ultimately a loss of power.

139

Buy The Truth and Sell It Not

Unfortunately, they neglected a very important judicial law of the Bible, and this lead to much confusion and error. Including the slaughter and persecution of Jews and Christians, who did not embrace the trinity. The judicial law of scripture tells us that every word must be established by at least two, if not three, witnesses (see Numbers 35:30, Deuteronomy 19:15, and II Corinthians 13:1). We learn that the crucifixion could not take place until Jesus confirmed His identity because the testimonies of the witnesses did not agree (see Mark 14:55-62).

This judicial law states that no one should be put to death by the testimony of one witness. We should follow this law when interpreting scripture, and determining what God's Biblical truth is. Neglecting to follow this law has resulted in a loss of power in much of Christianity. However, God did not allow the light of the Gospel to be entirely snuffed out. Our God is a consuming fire. In spite of human error, God's Spirit filled Church is still the most powerful force in this world.

As members of the body of Christ, we must hold fast to the truth. The world needs the demonstration of the Spirit like never before. We need a demonstration of the power of God in the perilous times we are living in. Every child of God should be endued with the power of the Holy Ghost. We must come to a place where we are not afraid to step out by faith, and reach out to people. The world cannot, and will not be reached inside of a building. The devil is attempting to infiltrate our minds with so much garbage, hoping we will not reach our potential.

However, the devil is not our biggest problem. We do not have to listen to him. Our biggest problem is what we chose to believe, and an unwillingness to fully submit to God. Sometimes we don't want to fully commit to God because we are afraid of what it will cost us. Some people don't want to change, so they back away from the truth, preferring to live a lie.

If we truly get close to God, we will be changed. Some don't want to die to their own will. It is the inherent fear of death in our flesh that keeps us from going the extra mile, making the additional sacrifice, and believing that God will do right by us no matter what. When the devil sees that an individual is lacks faith or is self willed, he knows he doesn't have to do much. They have already allowed their flesh to limit them. Those who are no threat to him, he typically leaves alone. Therefore, as children of God, if we have never had any resistance from the enemy, we might want to question our effectiveness in God's kingdom.

Our enemy does not trouble those with a worldly mindset, who do not seek God on a daily basis. Worldly thinking leads to strife, contention, and confusion. This mindset opened the door for error to come into the Church. Men argued over what should be taught until God's plan for salvation was edited according to man's philosophy. The result was a loss of much needed power. Unfortunately, mankind's questioning of God still goes on today. And is nothing short of rebellion and witchcraft. We must not allow the rudiments of this world to creep subtly into our minds.

We must be Spirit led, never forming our own personal views of God, others, and even ourselves that are not in accordance with God's Word. These mindsets are rooted in shame and fear. They lead to assumptions about situations and others that cause many breaches. Shame and fear are strongholds that must be brought under control in the life of every individual. Shame and pride, which are inherent in our humanity, are very similar. Shame may invoke feelings of humility, but in reality, our thoughts of unworthiness are in opposition to the mind of God.

Anytime we think we aren't worthy to do something or believe we can never be forgiven; we have just violated God's Word. His Word says that old things are passed away, and all things have become new. When we think like this, we don't believe that we have been born again. We make God's Word null and void in our lives. The truth of the matter is that God does love us, even if we are unlovable. When we are born again, we start out with no record. People might hold a record against us, but God does not. We should choose to believe the Word of God. We have to believe that God's love has made us worthy.

To overcome our insecurities, we must see ourselves through God's eyes. The only way to do this is to place value on ourselves. Calvary should be enough to show us how valuable we are. We must be of great value to God, or He wouldn't have died for us. One of the biggest problems with low self-esteem is that it affects how we act. Our fear of rejection can cause us to become deceived, and believe things that aren't true. We may even begin to believe things about God that aren't true.

It is a normal human desire to want to be loved and accepted, even by those who don't know God. We must not let fear of rejection stop us from standing for truth. We are admonished to earnestly contend for the faith that was once delivered to the saints (Jude 1:3). Those who are in covenant with God should be influencing those who don't know Him, not vying for worldly acceptance or being influenced by this world. When we are worried about being accepted by others, we run the risk of being influenced by the belief systems of those who we want to be approved by.

142

Buy The Truth and Sell It Not

We must be wise as serpents and gentle as doves, respecting others, and speaking the truth in love. Some will accuse those who stand for the truth of being judgmental, and not loving others. After all, they may say, "doesn't God love everyone"? "Doesn't the Bible say that nothing can separate us from the love of God"? But one might also ask, "How much do we love someone we do not share the Gospel with? And, while the Bible does give us a list of things that cannot separate us from the love of God, shame is not mentioned. Shame will separate us from God. God's love is unconditional, but we separate ourselves from God when we reject Him with unbelief.

If our relationship with God is a sure one, we will not be overly concerned with what others think about us. If we are focused on God, our priority will be to please Him. More than likely, we will not be able to change what someone thinks about us. Attempting to do so will often result in a violation of God's Word and principles. If we stand in our integrity, our actions will speak much louder than words. We are called to separation and holiness. Without love for others and ourselves, we cannot achieve holiness. This includes, first and foremost, our love for God. If God has a part in all we do, we will be holy. If we fail in this area, we cannot succeed in any other.

If we are to keep our covenant with God, who is a maker and keeper of covenants, our minds must be submitted to the laws of God. We cannot embrace worldly wisdom or doctrines man has created when it comes to our knowledge of God. All knowledge of God must be grounded in love, not fear or doubt. We must embrace perfect love, which casts out fear. This is the basis for all truth. Unconditional love does not come from worldly wisdom, and neither does forgiveness or repentance. These come from wisdom that can only come from God.

The Church must be vigilant because the spiritual forces that drove men into error are still at work today. As we approach the end of the age, this spirit is becoming more aggressive. The question that must be asked by every individual is, am I going to make a choice to submit my life completely to the Word of God, or will I choose to walk according to the mindset and philosophies of this world? God does not have to honor any ideologies that man has formed about Him. We are to be conformed to His image. He will not be conformed to our image. True Apostolic authority and power must be revived in our day. The Church at the end of the age will be greater than it was in the beginning (see Haggai 2:9, Ecclesiastes 7:9, James 5:7). The Church of today must pick up where the Apostles left off. We can be sure the enemy would like nothing more than to water down the Word and weaken the faith that was once given to the saints. The Church of today must earnestly contend for the truth of the Apostles doctrine. We must hold fast to the Gospel of Jesus Christ. It was the answer in the Apostles day, and it is the answer today for the problems in our society.

The Gospel is good news about the perfect love of a forgiving God, who sacrificed all for us. This was God's plan from the foundation of the world. By His death, burial, and resurrection; He defeated death, hell, and the grave. He came to deliver those in bondage to sin, shame, and fear. God never allowed Apostolic doctrine to to be lost. In spite of fear and unbelief, the Gospel continues to be preached to all nations. God's truth is available to all who will receive it.

Buy The Truth and Sell It Not

Sadly, not all are willing. History tells of a notable man whose unbelief lead to the formulation of a theory that teaches against God's existence. Trials, trauma, and discouraging situations have caused many to doubt God. This was the case with Charles Darwin, who is known as the father of the evolutional theory. "After watching his ten-year-old daughter, Annie, die of a painful disease, Charles Darwin found it nearly impossible to believe an all-powerful God could allow such a thing. The inability to reconcile a loving God and a world of suffering ultimately leads to despair and hopelessness" (answersingenesis.org). In our humanity, without the help of God, the result of despair and hopeless is doubt and fear.

In 1859, Darwin published his first book. "The full title of Darwin's most famous work included some stark words: On the Origin of Species by Means of Natural Selection, or the Preservation of Favored Races in the Struggle for Life. Darwin envisioned the spontaneous formation of simple life evolving into higher forms through the pitiless forces of nature selecting the fittest" (answersingenesis.org). Darwin questioned the existence of God after watching his daughter suffer. He couldn't understand how a loving God would allow pain and suffering. Thus we have the theory of evolution.

The theory of evolution is a doctrine that was birthed from one man's doubt, fear, and anger. This theory denies the existence of God. Also, it teaches something about mankind that the Bible does not. Evolution states that there are different races of people, evolving from an animal life form, some forms of persons being higher, and some being lower. This theory does not take into account the amount of melanin in a person's skin, and implies that some, which have darker skin, are closer to monkeys, which they allegedly evolved from. The higher forms, being white or Aryan, evolved into a higher life form.

While Darwin's theory, which is widely embraced and taught in schools, denies divine creation; the Bible teaches that all men are made in God's image (Genesis 1:26). All men came from the dust of the ground (Genesis 2:7), and all men are of one blood (see Acts 17:26). A great sacrifice was made for all men, regardless of their physical appearance or skin color (see John 3:16). God has not placed any man above another. All men are created equal, while there may be cultural differences, we have all descended from the sons of Noah.

While Darwin did not necessarily promote racism, "Darwinian evolution was (and still is) inherently a racist philosophy. It promotes a mindset that is in direct opposition to the Word of God. Evolution leaves our creator out, and gives no eternal hope of any kind. Evolution teaches that different groups or "races" of people evolved at different times and rates. (answersingenesis.org). The theory of evolution resulted in a great sin committed against God and mankind, known to us as racism. This evil has no place in God's Church. God will have a Church made up of every nation. Racism must not be allowed to dwell amongst us. It is an enemy of the Gospel of Jesus Christ.

Chapter Seven
The Restoration of All Things

God has called His Church to be His hands, feet, and voice in this world. As His ambassadors, we must work in His stead. This is the will of God, as God is not willing that any should perish. The opportunity for salvation has been made available to all of mankind. God is not a respecter of persons. He did not have one nation of people in mind when He went to Calvary. God told Abraham, who was a Jew, that he would be the father of many nations. How could this be possible? It is a promise kept that will continue to be fulfilled through the Gospel of Jesus Christ.

The Gospel will be preached to every nation. And will bring to pass the birth of the children promised to Abraham by faith (see Galatians 3:26-29). It is not God's will for segregation to be present in His Church. Revelation 14:6 says, *"And I saw another angel fly in the midst of heaven, having the everlasting Gospel to preach unto them that dwell on the earth, and to every nation, and kindred, and tongue, and people"*. It is God's will for everyone to have a chance to know Him. It is sinful to think that we should not have any person worship with us because of their skin color. Of course there will be cultural differences between people, but all have a purpose in His divine order. It is impossible for one nationality to reach every nation. Paul said he became all things to all people, that he might save some. Laborers from every nation are needed in God's Kingdom.

The Restoration of All Things

If God had intended for us all to be the same, He would not have confounded the languages at the tower of Babel. He would have just let mankind continue in their own way of doing things (see Genesis 11:9). They were of one mind; united against the will of God. We are given the impression they were building the tower because they didn't trust God. They had decided, as one segregated and disobedient people, to find their own way to heaven. We cannot be like them. We must not let fear of those who are different from us stop us from reaching every nation with the Gospel. We must show God's love to all mankind. The outer appearance, which God is not concerned with, should not be our concern. The color of our brother's skin should not determine if we consider them worthy of our fellowship.

On the other hand, if we bind together as one people to do the will of God, nothing can stand in our way. Not satan, who seeks to cause division, our feelings of unworthiness, or a fear of those who are different. We should not let fear of those who are different stand in the way of reaching out to the lost. How can we reach a lost and dying world if we are afraid of people because they are different from us? And how can we reach them if we shun them for these differences? While we know that Acts 2:38 is vital, we must remember something equally important. Loving our neighbor as ourselves is as important as obeying Act 2:38. If we do not have this revelation about our fellow man, then we have missed the message of the Gospel.

The message of the Gospel goes beyond the death, burial, and resurrection of our Lord and Savior. The Gospel should produce the peaceable fruit of righteousness, which compels us to love our neighbor as ourselves. If it has not, we have failed to understand the power of the cross, and we certainly do not know God or His Word. God has spoken throughout His Word that all of mankind has been created in His image. If we believe we are

148

better than someone else because of the color of their skin or economic status, we are insulting God. Didn't God create us all? Including the stranger, the widow, and the poor?

Evolution left creation out of its theory, and made it acceptable for some to treat their fellow man as animals; making abuse, discrimination, and even genocide acceptable. While Darwin cannot be held solely responsible for these things, he did influence Hitler, and others like him. After this teaching took root men's minds, and was combined with the inherent evil that can be found in men's hearts, it led to the evil of racism. Darwinian evolution taught a fallacy that claimed that different groups of people evolved at different times and rates, so some groups were not as evolved as others. Leading evolutionist Stephen Jay Gould claimed, "Biological arguments for racism may have been common before 1859, but they increased by orders of magnitude following the acceptance of evolutionary theory. The Australian Aborigines, for instance, were considered the missing links between the apelike ancestor, and the rest of mankind. This resulted in terrible prejudices and injustices towards the Australian Aborigines" (answersingenensis.org).

Evolutional thinking, which for all intensive purposes, can be labeled as fear based and rooted in disobedience; led those who embraced it, to separate themselves from God because of their prejudices and fear. This fearful thinking resulted in hatred towards their fellow man. History testifies of the crimes against humanity caused by racism. This "evolutionistic and humanistic" mindset was a catalyst for the actions of some, who believed it acceptable to exterminate their fellow man. It is common for our carnal man to want to eliminate, or exterminate something we fear. If we think of our fellow man as some lower life form, where will that lead? Most of us have no problem killing something we are afraid of or are okay with its demise.

The Restoration of All Things

The Word of God says that hatred of our brother is like murder (see I John 3:15). Hatred against our brother, who is of another nation, is sin, which is often motivated by fear. How many of us think nothing of killing a spider? Why? Because we are afraid of it, and want it gone. Even though we would never physically kill our brother, our fear, insecurities, and jealousies might slay him in our hearts. Our covenant relationship with God is dependent on our love for our brother. We can't love as God commands us, if we fear those who are not like us.

The following is an account of Ota Benga, a Pygmy man from Africa, who fell victim to science, evolution, and those that did not know God. Unbelievable cruelty was perpetrated on Benga, who was a Bushman, and was put on display with an orangutan in the Bronx Zoo. "The man who was put on display in a zoo was brought from the Belgian Congo in 1904 by noted African explorer Samuel Verner. The man, a pygmy named Ota Benga (or 'Bi', which meant 'friend' in his language), was soon presented by Verner to the Bronx Zoo director, William Hornaday. The pygmy was born in 1881 in Africa. When put in the zoo, he was 150 centimetres (4 feet 11 inches) tall, about 23 years old, and weighed a mere 47 kilos (103 pounds).

Often referred to as a boy, he had been actually married twice—his first wife had been kidnapped by a hostile tribe, and his second had died from a poisonous snake bite" (answersingenesis.org). The end result of this man being captured, sold, and brought to the United States is tragic.

Through ignorance, he had been given companions to keep him happy (a parrot and an orangutan). Sadly, it was widely believed at that time that blacks were evolutionarily inferior to whites. This belief resulted in the cruelty of the Benga exhibit, and his being treated like an animal. The Benga exhibit became a cause for much negative publicity. This led to an uproar among some local ministers, who rather than being appalled by the cruelty, feared that the Benga exhibit might give credence to, and be used to prove the Darwinian Evolutionary theory.

With the threat of legal action, the zoo director decided it was better to let Benga out of the cage. Benga walked the zoo grounds in a white suit during the day, returning to the monkey house at night. He was often followed by crowds and laughed at. He began to hate being mobbed by these crowds who came to gawk at him. The sad situation escalated to the point where Benga had to be removed from the park. The New York Times of September 18, 1906, described the problem: "There were 40,000 visitors to the park on Sunday. Nearly every man, woman and child of this crowd made for the monkey house to see the star attraction in the park—the wild man from Africa. They chased him about the grounds all day, howling, jeering, and yelling. Some of them poked him in the ribs, others tripped him up, all laughed at him" (answersingenesis.org).

After these things, Benga became violent, and in an effort to protect himself from his tormentors, made a small bow and arrow from things he found in the park. He ended up wounding some people, who were particularly tormenting him. It was decided it would be best if he left the park. After leaving the park, he was able to find care at some institutions, and with some sympathetic individuals. Sadly, Benga was never able to shed his "Freak" label. While working in a tobacco factory in Lynchburg Virginia, he became increasingly depressed. Realizing he would never return to his native land, he ended up committing suicide in 1916 with a borrowed gun. There are many published articles that tell of Benga's plight at the hands of his fellow man (accounts vary). There is also a book called, *The Pygmy in The Zoo*, written by Phillip Verner Bradford.

The Restoration of All Things

Benga's treatment, after being removed from his native land, demonstrated the acts of people who have no knowledge of God, or love for their fellow man. Those of us that know Him must have love for our neighbor, and not consider ourselves to be better than anyone else. We must count all men worthy of hearing the Gospel of Jesus Christ. Scientific theories that teach against the Word of God led to this evil.

What a shame that those, who were aware of his situation, claiming Christianity, did not band together for their fellow man. His plight might have been averted, and his end different. It is noteworthy that the Christians of Ota Benga's day took notice of the correlation that exists between the theory of evolution and racism. It was their fear of Ota Benga's physical appearance confirming Darwin's theory that brought about his release from the cage at the zoo.

However, their lack of concern for Ota Benga's well being revealed the true condition of their hearts. Thankfully, we have missionaries who will risk their lives, sacrificing all, to take the good news of the Gospel of Jesus Christ to all nations. It is this truth that makes all men free; where all are created in God's image, and all are one in Jesus Christ. Although Benga was a soul that Jesus died for, no mention was ever made regarding concern for his soul. Those outside the Church, regardless of their lifestyle, nationality, or financial status, are souls that Christ died for (see John 3:16).

We might not embrace our neighbor's lifestyle, but we should be wiling to share the Gospel. We must welcome them into God's Church with open arms, should the opportunity present itself. We must not fear contamination from sin, or have hatred in our hearts for the lost of any nation. Those who have been covered in the blood of Jesus through water baptism, and filled with the Holy Ghost should be able to boldly take authority over the things of this world.

We are ambassadors of Christ, who overcame the world. It is the will of God that all nations hear the Gospel. God, who keeps His promises, promised faithful Abraham, that through him, all the families of the earth would be blessed (see Genesis 12:3). Why was Abraham, who was once Abram, called faithful? The Bible says that Abraham believed God, and as a result, obeyed God. His obedience was accounted to him as righteousness. He received a name change, Abraham means "father of many nations". Abraham was not a fearful man. He was not a perfect man, but he had faith.

The men who developed evolutional theories were fearful men. One such theory by Ernst Haeckel, "ontogeny recapitulates phylogeny" claimed: "At the lowest stage of human mental development are the Australians, some tribes of the Polynesians, and the Bushmen, Hottentots, and some of the Negro tribes. Nothing, however, is perhaps more remarkable in this respect, than that some of the wildest tribes in southern Asia and eastern Africa have no trace whatever of the first foundations of all human civilization, of family life, and marriage. They live together in herds, like apes". (answersingenesis.org).

Haeckel's theory, which is now discredited, later became known as the recapitulation theory. Ontogeny is the growth (size change) and development (shape change) of an individual organism, while phylogeny is said to be the evolutionary history of a species. This teaching along with Darwin's, "survival of the fittest" not only left God out of creation, but led men to embrace a mindset that God did not want Adam and Eve to have. A mindset that they did not need God. Humanism is at the root of all racism. And has led to a disregard for human life.

The Restoration of All Things

As in the days of Noah, the earth is filled with violence. Murder is not uncommon, and many do not fear God. While many speak against racism, claiming they are being discriminated against, racism is still very prevalent in **all** nationalities. Racism should not be found in any of God's Churches. Racism is a violation of the Word of God. Job is possibly one of the oldest books of the Bible. Job, being a man who sought after God, and His righteousness said, *"If I did despise the cause of my manservant or of my maidservant, when they contended with me; What then shall I do when God riseth up? and when he visiteth, what shall I answer him? Did not he that made me in the womb make him? and did not one fashion us in the womb" (Job 31:13-15)?* If Job is indeed the oldest book in the Bible, it was written before the law of Moses, and the prophets. This informs us that racism was a problem even then, and has always been abominable to God. Job, who feared God, heard from God concerning the treatment of his fellow man. He also knew He would stand in judgment for any bias towards his brother. He knew that one creator made all of mankind.

The early Church, who embraced Acts 2:38, had the revelation that keeping slaves was wrong. It was done away with in God's Church because it went against Biblical teaching. The Word of God clearly states that all men are created in God's image, and stand equal before Him (see Colossians 3:11, Galatians 3:28). Those who owned slaves within the early Church, who experienced inward conversion, chose to set them free. As a result, those outside the Church saw evidence of their inward conversion. There were other believers later on who followed suit. One example is John Newton, the writer of the song Amazing Grace. Newton became an abolitionist after his conversion to Christ.

154

The Restoration of All Things

None of our Churches should be a place where anyone of another nation does not belong. It is written, as you have done unto the least of these, you have also done unto me. Scientists have found through studies of DNA, that biologically there is only one race of humans. The human race. Genetic differences of outward appearance account for only a small percentage between nationalities as the following chart demonstrates.

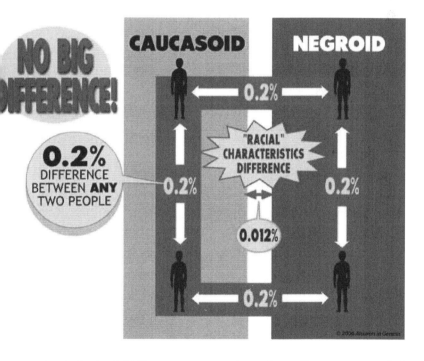

The belief of different races other than "homo sapien" (human race) is not only Biblically, but scientifically incorrect". In a recent interview on Comedy Central's The Nightly Show, host Larry Wilmore, asked TV's popular Bill Nye "The Science Guy" this question, "Does racism exist in the animal kingdom?" In Nye's reply, he made this statement, "We're all the same . . . from

155

a scientific standpoint there's no such thing as race". Bill Nye's answer showed us how much science has changed its position when it comes to the idea of different human races.

Actually, this part of Nye's answer is much more a Biblical than evolutionary view of humanity. As stated earlier, evolutional theories, which are rooted in man's fear and disobedience, have led to crimes against humanity, and the violation of God's greatest commandment. What should be most important to us is how God sees us treating our neighbor on a day to day basis. What does He think when we pass someone on the street, while driving in our car, standing in line at the store, and so on? We are commanded not only to love God, but also our neighbor. Jesus was questioned by a certain lawyer, who wanted to know who he was required to love. Jesus answered with the parable we know as The Good Samaritan.

It has been preached from our pulpits, and taught in Sunday School for many years. According to Strong's Concordance outline of Biblical usage, the word "neighbour" means: "a. a friend, b. any other person, where two are concerned, (thy fellow man, thy neighbor), according to the Jews, any member of the Hebrew nation and commonwealth. c. According to Christ, any other man irrespective of nation or religion with whom we chance to meet" (Strong's Online Concordance). It is sad enough if those outside God's Church embrace racist beliefs. But if we who belong to Christ, oppose Him concerning our neighbor, we can be certain that He will hold us to His standards.

God, who is never left without a witness to His righteousness, greatness, goodness, and loving kindness, came in the form of man to right all wrongs, stating that all are created equal. Galatians 3:28-29 says, *"There is neither Jew nor Greek, there is neither bond nor free, there is neither male nor female: for ye are all one in Christ Jesus. And if ye be Christ's, then are ye Abraham's seed, and heirs according to the promise".* God does not put differences between different ethnicities. Nor does He approve segregation. In Acts 10, God saw the heart of a man from another nation who was devout. Because of this man's faithfulness, Peter was sent a vision.

This vision was God's way of telling Peter he was to spread the Gospel to all nations. In this vision, Peter saw a sheet, that represented a vessel, knit at four corners, coming down from heaven to the earth, and raising back up. This was repeated three times. Could it be that God was showing Peter the four corners of the earth; north, south, east, and west? It is interesting to note that the word "knit", which is used in Acts 10:11, implies unity in the original language used.

According to the online Theological Dictionary of the New Testament, two meanings in Greek are, "to cause to coalesce, and put together in one's mind", "to cause a person to unite with one in a conclusion or come to the same opinion". The vessel in Peter's vision was full of beasts that were unclean to the Jews. After descending, the vessel was brought back up to heaven. This is symbolic to all nations being acceptable to God. It can also symbolize the three days that Jesus was buried and resurrected. However, we know that Peter heard a voice saying, *"Rise Peter; kill and eat" (Acts 10:13).* Peter refused, saying, I have never eaten anything common or unclean. The voice spoke again saying, *"What God hath cleansed, that call not thou common"* (Acts 10:15). God is able to cleanse any heart, and His blood removes all sin. Faith is what makes all men righteous in His eyes. Racism has its roots in fear and unbelief. How can we say we love God if we question the existence of our brother? In doing so, we question the very existence of God, and we question His creative power. There is no greater enemy to revival than racism. The will of God cannot be accomplished until this evil is put under our feet. It should never be found amongst those who claim Christianity. The term race needs to be done away with in regards to different nations. Biblically and scientifically there is one race, the human race. God commanded Israel to love the stranger (see Deuteronomy 10:19). They were told not to oppress the stranger because they knew how it felt to be oppressed. They were instructed to have compassion because of their days of slavery in Egypt (see Exodus 23:9). We should remember where we came from, and not consider anyone to be an outsider.

Those of us who were blessed to be raised in God's Church may have never known the bad effects of the world. Even so, shouldn't God's Church have the compassion He has on the lost, regardless of nationality or economic background? We are called to be a powerful force against the enemy, and to be one in the unity of the Spirit. God hates discrimination. While there are many examples to confirm this, the most notable is when Miriam came with Aaron to confront Moses because he had married an Ethiopian woman. Numbers 12:1 says, *"And Miriam and Aaron spake against Moses because of the Ethiopian woman whom he had married: for he had married an Ethiopian woman"*. It has been said that God was angry because Moses' authority was being questioned. This may be true, but Numbers 12:1 specifies, *"for he had married an Ethiopian woman"*.

The reason for their complaint, which Miriam appears to have initiated first, was because of the Ethiopian woman he had married. The Bible says the anger of the Lord was kindled against them because of this. Although both Miriam and Aaron approached Moses, Miriam was the one struck with leprosy. Possibly because God saw the condition of her heart.

Aaron repented immediately, according to the scripture, which says, *"And Aaron said unto Moses, Alas, my lord, I beseech thee, lay not the sin upon us, wherein we have done foolishly, and wherein we have sinned"* (Numbers 12:11). It should be noted that Aaron did not call their discrimination a difference of opinion. He clearly called it sin, asking for forgiveness. There is no record of Miriam's repentance. Aaron interceded on Miriam's behalf, and God said, let her be shut out of the camp seven days. Everything unclean was shut outside of the camp. Lepers were shut out so they would not contaminate the congregation. Presumably Miriam was healed afterwards, but nothing more is said about Miriam until her death.

While God did command His people not to intermingle with other nations because they served other gods. There is no scripture against marriage unions between those of different nations who are of like faith. Although he was loved by God, King Solomon's marriages to strange women were his downfall. While scripture teaches against unequal yokes as they pertain to faith, some have misinterpreted these scriptures to mean that those of different nationalities should not marry. We do not see interracial marriage spoken against in scripture.

Rahab was of a different nation than Israel, but her nationality did not matter. Her faith did. When we first hear of Rahab, a Canaanite, she was a harlot. It was because of her faith in God that she was saved. Her faithfulness also saved her family. This Rahab is believed to be the same Rahab later named in the genealogy of Jesus (see Matthew 1:5). Her faith brought her out of her sinful situation, and took her away from the background she came from. The Canaanites were known to be ungodly, and were cursed because of their sinful nature.

God doesn't look upon the outward appearance. He looks at the heart. Rahab, in order to have been named in the lineage of Jesus, must have married a descendent of Shem, who we know to be of Jewish descent. Ruth is another woman who stands out as a woman of faith. Although, she came from an ungodly background, her faithfulness, and desire of follow the true God of Israel made her eligible to marry Boaz.

Scripture tells us that Moab was cursed forever for not allowing the children of Israel to pass through their land (see Judges 11:17, and Jeremiah 48:42). While Moab as a whole is cursed, apparently God does not discriminate against those who are willing to separate themselves, and follow Him. This includes marriage to fellow believers, regardless of their nationality. There is no clearer demonstration of the love and justice of God than this. Ruth and Naomi's stories let us know that it doesn't matter where someone came from, in God's Kingdom all are made equal.

Again, we are admonished not to be unequally yoked with unbelievers regardless of nationality (see II Corinthians 6:14). Nationally is not the issue. We are all one in Christ. This is demonstrated in many ways in the book of Acts, and in the epistles written to the Church. Any other way of thinking is not from God. When Peter had his vision in Acts 10, he was given revelation on the rooftop. With this revelation came the awareness that God was doing a new thing regarding people of faith from nations other than Israel. Peter also received a greater revelation about the power of salvation as it pertains to all mankind. Acts 10:28 says, *"And he said unto them, Ye know how that it is an unlawful thing for a man that is a Jew to keep company, or come unto one of another nation; but God hath shewed me that I should not call any man common or unclean"*.

In Peter's day there may have been other reasons for segregation from other nations, but the most notable reason was faith. In our day, there is war between Israel and Palestine over land that was Biblically given to Israel when David slew the Goliath. What is going on over there in our day has spiritual implications regarding faith. Some believe that what happened at the World Trade Center on 9/11 had nothing to do with faith, but it is apparent that it did. It brought a nation together, and caused its citizens to turn towards God for a moment in time. There was a fear of the unknown that was a wake up call. Will it take something catastrophic to cause us to draw near to God?

Our faith must be strong, we cannot succumb to fear, and we must never cast God's promises aside. Can loss, or fear of the unknown, make us break our covenant with God? Will the things we suffer in this life convince us that God doesn't love us? If some are willing to die for a false god, what is to be said of those that walk out on God because something doesn't go their way or because of loss?

We cannot minimize loss, especially of loved ones, but those who hold onto God in spite of loss are those who overcome. Their lives testify of the power, greatness, and reality of God. Our convictions must be more powerful than our fears. When we put our love for God first, we will not be overcome by fear. We will not turn our backs on Him when we face tragedy or loss. Darwin's theory of evolution was birthed in part from what he learned from his father, then nurtured by fear, depression, suffering, and loss.

The theory of evolution was birthed in his mind due to his own illness, and then became his faith after the death of his daughter. After his death, these words were found in his writings, "I can indeed hardly see how anyone ought to wish Christianity to be true; for if so the plain language of the text seems to show that the men who do not believe, and this would include my father, brother and almost all my best friends, will be everlastingly punished. And this is a damnable doctrine" (answersingenesis.org). Darwin's mindset, and the theory of evolution, were birthed as a result of life's tragedies, and are very much in line with the teaching of humanism.

We must be careful not to cast doubt on God's goodness because of the bad things that happen in this world. As was stated early on, mankind allowed satan to have dominion. Looking back to what satan said to Eve, we know that he cast doubt on what God said in an attempt to make God look unjust. The enemy put the thought in her mind that God had not only lied to her, but that He was withholding something good from her. At that time Eve forgot about what she had (an existence in paradise where there was no pain, suffering, or death), and became focused on the one thing she didn't have. Her covetousness caused her to seek knowledge that God never intended for her to have, knowledge of evil, and a desire for knowledge of things that must be accepted by faith.

This original breach of covenant caused a loss of innocence in mankind that was not present at his creation. Hence fear, sin, and shame entered in. And the battle with rebellion began. Sadly, for some, this is a battle they have already conceded to through deception, and the belief that their ways are better than God's. We must not let ourselves fall into the same trap. When satan made his first appearance in the garden, he attempted to steal man's faith, and his tactics haven't changed. However, since sickness and death entered the world, our enemy has much more to work with than he had with Adam and Eve. Before the fall, it would appear that mankind had no knowledge of death, spiritual or otherwise.

Most of us would admit that the thought of losing a loved one is bad enough, but the thought of them being lost is unbearable. Even so, we cannot let go of our faith because if we believe that God is a righteous judge, then we must let our minds be at peace, knowing that they are in the hands of a righteous and loving God. We cannot minimize the loss of loved ones, and must accept God's sovereignty by faith. Admittedly, this is easier said than done. However, in the long run, it is the only way to make it. As always, we must always leave the judgment of all things to God.

We can do this because in every situation God is good. We love Him because we believe He first loved us. If fear takes hold in our hearts, no good will come from it. Sometimes we will go through pain and loss in this world. It is at times like these when we need God more than ever. If we allow fear to manifest its ugly face in our lives, we will be brought to the pit of despair, and possibly hell. Fearing the loss of our loved ones should never turn us away from God. Our fears should be turned to prayers of faith for their salvation. We can turn the table on fear, and pray and fast for them like never before. We must choose to believe in the love and goodness of God.

God's perfect love will always cast out fear. The time to praise God is not only when things are going great, but in times of adversity. We must choose to exercise our faith. We must look to the light when things are dark, and we can't see the way before us. He must be a light unto our path, not only in Word, but in deed. Glorifying God should always be in the forefront of our mind, even when we face a terrible situation. Maybe the most we can do is call on His name.

In those times, that is enough. He always draws near at the mention of His name. He is an ever present help in our time of need. Our actions must demonstrate to the world, and to the enemy, that we believe He is God. We must be able to bring His Word to life by putting it into practice when something bad happens to us. This is one of the ways that the people, who know their God, do exploits. The faith of God's people is what this world needs to see because we are living in a time when men's hearts are gripped by fear.

The whole creation is groaning for the manifestation of the sons of God. What will draw them more than those who have answers for them? When they see our faith persevere in the midst of dark times, they will come to us because of the power of our God. This world needs the Spirit of God to shine in the darkness. We must be that city that is set upon a hill. God foresaw these days of darkness when Joel prophesied the promise that God would pour out His Spirit on all flesh. It is coming to pass in our lifetime. We know by looking around us that perilous times are indeed here.

As the bride of Christ, we must be preparing for His return. God's people must be filled and led by the Holy Ghost, not by the spirit of fear. We must be determined to walk in the Spirit everyday, praying with our "most holy faith", if we are to do the will of God. When Jesus was asked by some who wanted to know how to "work the works of God", His answer was simple, but requires commitment. The Bible tell us that *"Jesus answered and said unto them, This is the work of God, that ye believe on him whom he hath sent"* (John 6:29). Jesus was presumably talking to the Jews of His day, but the message is the same for all. We must fight the good fight of faith.

We are living in perilous times. We cannot overcome without faith. Many men are lovers of themselves, idolizing everything but God. Those who we should be able to look up to are boastful and proud. Children are raised without the knowledge of God, and have no respect for their parents. The following admonition should cause those who fear God to seek an altar of prayer. It is a reminder of the hour we are living in. And should convict Christians everywhere to seek God every day, with the understanding that we must embrace the power of God in our lives, with a love for truth.

Truth will illuminate the enemies' strategies. The Bible tells us in II Timothy 3:5, that there will be those who will turn away from a true covenant relationship with God. Instead of being powerful, they will have "a form of godliness". In other words, they will have the appearance of believers, but their lives will not be changed. They will meet on Sundays, maybe during the week, but will remain unchanged. Those with a "form of godliness" cannot change the atmosphere around them. Paul was talking to the Church when he gave this admonition. We must be sure that the fear of coming out of our comfort zones isn't causing us to walk with a "form of godliness", forsaking the power needed to witness to this world. We must examine every area of our lives to make sure we are walking in faith.

Fear indeed has many faces, which manifest according to what is most detrimental to each individual. The enemy has been witness to every bad thing that has happened to us all our lives. The good news is that God was also there. All knowing, and all powerful. Man originally gave the enemy space to walk to and fro in this earth when he sinned, but God had a plan. From the foundation of the world, God planned to become flesh, and never leave us through the power of the Holy Ghost. He gives us power to overcome the prince of this world. Our faith is a necessary ingredient to our covenant relationship with God because faith is evidence of our love for God.

Faith is obedience. Remembering that fear or unbelief translated in the original language implies disobedience, we can see how listening to, and embracing the voice of fear is sin. When we question everything that happens; not accepting by faith the Word God has given us to live by, we question God's love for us. If we question His love for us, we cannot love and obey Him as we should. Where there is distrust, love cannot do its perfect work. We cannot even pray effectively when we doubt God's love for us. It is hard enough to love someone we can't see, but loving someone who we don't believe loves us is even more difficult.

Our covenant relationship with God must be built on trust. We might not be able to attain unto God's love and faithfulness in our humanity, but we can make the decision to allow our actions to demonstrate our love for God. Our love and obedience is more important than anything else to God. When we accept God's perfect love; fear of failure, fear of rejection, fear of man, of loneliness, of loss, of death, and whatever else is cast out. To love God, we must know Him, and to know Him, we must learn to think like Him. This requires believing His Word, and seeking His face more than we seek His hand. We must seek His face to know Him. We must know Him in order to accomplish what He has called us to do. God has a purpose and plan for us that cannot be accomplished if we are not obedient to His Word.

In these perilous times, there will be battles, but we are promised the victory if we are on God's side. In the prophecy given to Daniel, the Bible says, *"And such as do wickedly against the covenant shall he corrupt by flatteries: but the people that do know their God shall be strong, and do exploits".* (Daniel 11:32) When we are obedient to the Word of God, He will not allow us to be deceived. We will be bold as lions when we stand in righteousness. An "exploit" is a bold or daring feat. The early Church was powerful, and accomplished many exploits. They often faced persecution. Persecution from those that opposed them prompted a prayer meeting.

As a result, they were filled again with the Holy Ghost, and spoke the Word boldly (see Acts 4). Instead of running in fear when they faced a situation, they had faith to pray because they knew God would answer. This is how they were able to achieve the exploits we read about. They knew the power of God. The word "strong" in Hebrew, used in the book of Daniel, means to bind, restrain, and conquer. When we are in covenant with God, we are able to overcome the world as He has. When we are motivated by faith, we are able to bind the forces of darkness, and loose the power of heaven. Not only into our situation, but into the lives of others, thereby increasing their faith. Jesus said, *"whatever you bind on earth will be bound in heaven, and whatever is loosed on earth, will be loosed in heaven"*.

We live in a world that is hurting. God's Church must continue the work Jesus began. Jesus said we would not only do the works He did, but do greater works. The word "greater" literally means more. The called of the Lord should be reaching every nation. We must work while it is day because the night is coming when no man can work. We must be a light in a dark world. Multitudes of people came to Jesus because He taught them, encouraged them, healed their diseases, and loved them. Revival in all nations will happen when God's perfect love is manifested in our lives. We must stand in faith, testifying boldly with wisdom, regardless of the scare tactics of the enemy. We will not be deceived, if we seek the face our Lord and Savior, Jesus Christ. So, let us consider the conclusion of the whole matter. "Fear God, and keep His commandments". And we can be sure we will find restoration for our souls.

Works Cited

Http://americanhumanist.org/Humanism". Interview. Weblog post. N.p., n.d. Web.

Https://answersingenesis.org/racism/are-there-really-different-races/". Weblog post. N.p., n.d. Web.

Weblog post. Https://answersingenesis.org/charles-darwin/racism/did-darwin-promote-racism/. N.p., n.d. Web. Weblog post. N.p., n.d. Web.

Weblog post. Http://www.eliyah.com/lexicon.html. N.p., n.d. Web.

Quasten, Johannes. *Patrology*. 4 Vols. Thomas More Pr, U.S.A., 1999.

All scripture has been taken from the King James Version of the Bible.

All Greek and Hebrew definitions were taken from Strong's Online Concordance, unless otherwise noted.

Please note:

All information, other than that written by the author, was taken from the internet over a period of eight years. All were and are public domain. Due to the time span, dates are not included, as these articles or information may or may not still be available online. All have been noted to give credit here or within the text.